TO FRANCE – WITH LOVE!

# To France – With Love!

*by*

## Paddy King-Fretts

The Pentland Press Limited
Edinburgh · Cambridge · Durham · USA

First published in 2000 by
The Pentland Press Ltd.
1 Hutton Close
South Church
Bishop Auckland
Durham

British Library Cataloguing in Publication Data.
A catalogue record for this book is available
from the British Library.

ISBN 1 85821 745 8

Typeset by George Wishart & Associates, Whitley Bay.
Printed and bound by Antony Rowe Ltd., Chippenham.

*To*
*Hugo, Jamie, Daniel and Tristan*

# Contents

# List of Illustrations

# *Preface*

I had not the slightest intention of recording our adventure when we set out from England in late 1992. Rachel had kept a diary for a number of years and I was happy that it would be sufficient if ever we wished to refer back to the past and recall some incident or other. Furthermore, I have never found writing easy and throughout my life have, wherever possible, avoided having to produce anything more comprehensive than the shortest possible memo. Yet now, after a year of application *To France – with Love!* has appeared. How so?

Our very first house guest – Bill Foster – warned us that people would want to know about our story. As a professional journalist he saw a tale that would, if properly recorded, fascinate all those who loved the idea of a holiday or a home in France and urged us to seriously consider keeping a record of events. This has been echoed time and again by all our guests who, together with so many of our French friends, have been captivated by the spirit of our adventure and, throughout their time at Bosc Lebat, have quizzed us remorselessly about our lives in France and why we came here. Eventually I got the message that our little story, although similar to many others, caught the imagination and held a fascination for so many.

Surely, I thought, a tale such as ours has been recorded already – others must have been encouraged to write about their adventures. There have been a number of British books about France, life in France and the age old Anglo-French relationship. Some are household names, others virtually unknown, but as far as we can tell there has not been a book about setting up and running a holiday business. It is an every day story – thousands have done the same as us, yet every tale is different and ours is no exception.

*To France – with Love!* is the record of our story. I have tried to give as balanced an account as possible, recording our moments of drama, luck, despair; our worries, our hopes and expectations; our difficult times and the moments of pure magic. It begins when Rachel and I met in Winchester and ends some time in the recent past – it is but a chapter and I would ask the reader to view it as such. Time has moved on and already new events, some monumental, others of little significance, have woven fresh patterns in our lives.

Bosc Lebat
*Autumn 1999*

# *Foreword*

*by*

**Sir Peter de la Billiere**

'To France – With Love!' brings back many fond memories of happy visits to Bosc Lebat and, in particular, of the author – Paddy King-Fretts. I first met Paddy many years ago when he joined the Regiment at Hereford as a young Troop Commander. Later, when the fighting in Oman was at its height, I persuaded the Ministry of Defence to release him so that he could serve with me again when I was Commanding Officer. He left the Army in 1992 and, with his wife Rachel, set out for France and their new lifestyle. This book is the story of that adventure.

Beginning from the time Paddy and Rachel first met in Winchester, the book tells how they found their new home and then restored Bosc Lebat, a beautiful manor house, into a small but exclusive holiday business. It is a lively story, filled with numerous moments of high drama, hard graft, hilarity, luck and – ultimately – success. This is a human tale that recounts the enormous difficulties and problems that had to be faced and overcome before their dream was realised.

Paddy is a great raconteur and has the unusual gift of being able to write as well as he speaks. Sometimes I found myself laughing out loud, on other occasions I was left wondering how they coped with all they had taken on. It is also a romance, something of a fairy tale, about which so many of us who remain caught up in the problems and hassles of every day life, can only dream. Finally, above all else, 'To France – With Love!' is a delightful read for all those who are considering settling in France, holidaying there or who are merely dreaming about it all.

*Peter de la Billiere*

# CHAPTER I

# France and the Army Days

I looked across the ditch and caught the eye of the French Officer.
Gerard Lemain did not fit the tough, aggressive mould of Les Paras.
His fine, slim features and high brow reminded me more of an academic
than a professional paratrooper. However, I had heard enough about
Gerard – the French Liaison Officer at the School of Infantry – to know
that underneath his mild, well-groomed exterior was an experienced
combat soldier who had won his spurs many times over in North and
Central Africa.

We had first met the previous year, in late 1989, when he had joined
the school and had come over to introduce himself to me. I was
commanding the Heavy Weapons Division and Gerard had expressed a
keen interest in learning how we went about our business.

I soon grew to like him and he would often escape from his office
at Warminster, drive across Salisbury Plain to my camp at Netheravon
and spend the day with us. He, his wife Marie-Claire and I had been
out together on a number of occasions, usually driving over to one
of the pubs on the River Test for supper and I had spent several
pleasant evenings with them in their little rented house close to
Warminster.

Gerard came from the elite Parachute Regiment – Le 1er RCP –
whose base was close to Bayonne on the south-west coast of France not
far from the Spanish border. I had worked with this unit some years
previously and admired their professional approach to soldiering.
Having been to France on a number of occasions, I confessed to Gerard,

not long after we met, how highly I regarded his country and that, perhaps one day, I would try to settle there.

Today he had slipped away from his office once again under the pretext of watching some of our heavy weapons firing. We had driven out to the ranges together and watched the last hour of activity before lunch. It was quiet now that they had all returned to camp and we sat in the lee of a high bank with the warm May sun on our backs, our packed lunches and thermos of coffee. Just the two of us together we forgot the formalities and chatted away easily like old friends.

'So you really are serious about France then?' he quizzed.

'Yes, I suppose I am. Its been on my mind for some time, especially now that these manpower cuts seem to be on their way,' I replied, then added hastily, 'but there's a lot to think about first.'

'That's for sure – and it's a big place too. When did you first get the idea?'

'Oh, that was years ago, way back in 1962, just after I had left Sandhurst. My regiment was in Plymouth down in Devon, waiting for something to come up and they decided to send me off on an adventure – to get some hairs on my chest, as they say.'

Gerard laughed, 'We were in Djibouti then and there was plenty going on there to get our chests hairy. But go on, tell me that they sent you to France for an adventure.'

He laughed loudly again but I knew he was fascinated about this great affection I had for his country and where it had all begun. On a number of occasions he had asked me to tell him the story and now we had a good hour to ourselves before the soldiers were due to return.

'Well, it's not a bad old yarn, we had a great time too.' With that I launched into the tale I remembered so well, even after nearly thirty years.

I had only just joined the regiment and, like all new officers I was keeping my head down, trying to keep out of the way and find my feet quietly. One day I was summoned to the HQ. It was a place to be avoided at all costs by very junior officers: I sensed that trouble lay ahead and wondered what was wrong. The Second in Command, after calling me into his office, asked quietly if I had ever done any canoeing and if I had ever been to France. I explained rather shamefaced that I had done neither and began wondering what sort of trap had been set for me when he said that he wanted me to do both.

He told me that he wanted me to take a party of soldiers over to France and cross the country from Le Havre to Marseilles by canoe. I stared at him in amazement but he seemed quite serious about it, telling me I had just two months to get the show on the road.

That got me out of the chair and for the next few weeks I was dashing around the place like a mad thing getting the team together, finding all the kit and doing as much training as we could. Known ironically as Exercise Massif, the paddling bit was to be just over 1,400 kilometres and I had been given six weeks to get there and back – and not a day longer if you don't mind! It was a hectic scramble but eventually we got going on 21 September, catching the night ferry over to Le Havre and, early the next morning, put the canoes into the water – to the amusement of a crowd of dockers who thought they had seen it all until our show began.

A glance at any map or chart will show you that a major international port such as Le Havre is a very big place indeed. When viewed from the bottom of a small and overloaded canoe bobbing around amongst all the harbour traffic it is an awesome sight. People can hardly see you and, even if they can, they expect you to get out of the way. There was an awful lot of traffic around on that first morning and we had a tricky time making our way in and out of it all before we reached the canal that links the harbour to the Seine.

It was a long and hard initial slog, the worst problem being the huge barges that came straight at us, pushing walls of water in front of them. Once they had passed there was a raging backwash that threw us all over the place often dashing the boats onto the rocks at the side of the canal. One or two were manageable but when ten or a dozen ganged up against our four little canoes nerves were tested. Our first day on the water was little more than a frantic battle for survival.

We pushed on as best we could and next morning tackled the huge lock leading onto the river. It was somewhat daunting being entombed in the well of the enormous lock sitting in the canvas boats alongside these great barges. As the water went down, the sides of the lock towered above us like the walls of a cathedral, water cascading down and we felt helpless and vulnerable – matchboxes waiting to be crushed. We were glad to get shot of the place and out onto the river where we could at least get some sort of routine going. Our first destination was Rouen then on to Paris.

September 28th – my twenty-first birthday – heralded the first of our dramas. By now we were anxious to get a lift on a barge for here the river was filthy and it was becoming increasingly difficult to find anywhere to pull in and camp for the night. An old barge went slowly past trailing an assortment of ropes in the water. We chased after it and the first one caught hold of a rope which was then tied to the second boat as it came alongside. The first canoe spun in the backwash and capsized leaving the one that was tied to be pulled away by the barge, the front man unable to reach the knot that secured him.

It was a right old pickle and we floundered around in the water making frantic efforts to get the canoe, the two men and as much equipment as we could ashore before the next barge came along. The banks were steep, the kit heavy and it was pouring with rain – a great day for a birthday! Finally, long after dark we got ourselves into some sort of order and crashed out exhausted. After a paddle of some ten miles the following morning, we found the other two waiting patiently for us at the next lock.

Eventually we got our lift with two splendid old boys who had been prisoners of the Germans in the War and who, once they knew we were British soldiers, made a huge fuss of us. We reached Paris on 1 October and made our way into the centre of the city just after dawn; something I will never forget.

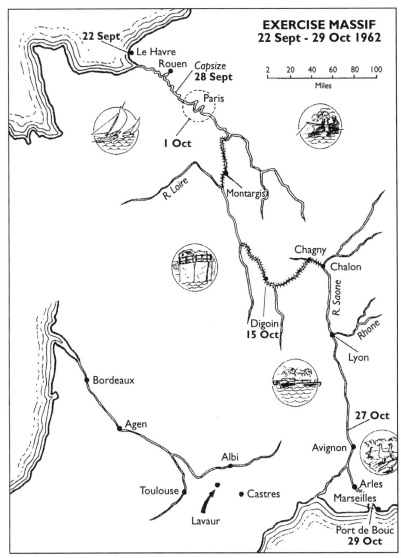

**EXERCISE MASSIF**
**22 Sept - 29 Oct 1962**

22 Sept

Le Havre

Rouen *Capsize*
**28 Sept**

Paris

**I Oct**

2  20  40  60  80  100
Miles

R. Loire

Montargis

Chagny

Chalon

R. Saone

Rhone

Digoin
**15 Oct**

Lyon

Bordeaux

Agen

**27 Oct**

Albi

Avignon

Toulouse · Castres

Arles
Marseilles

Lavaur

Port de Bouc
**29 Oct**

*Map of canoe trip – Exercise Massif.*

5

It was a beautiful sunny morning with a slight nip in the air. The leaves on the trees along the river bank were just turning and there were few folk about at this early hour. As the barge chugged slowly under the famous bridges, we sat together in silence, taking in the magnificent spectacle until we pulled in to the side and stopped near Notre Dame. Here we bade farewell to our kind hosts spending the next forty-eight hours on shore leave in the capital before pressing on further south.

It was a long hard slog down to the Loire valley and we took more than a week to reach the viaduct over the great river. Luckily the vast majority of lock-keepers and bargees treated us kindly and did whatever they could to help, often letting us through the locks ahead of the river traffic. Once they knew we were British soldiers en route to Marseilles the lock-keepers and their families spoiled us shamefully. Food and wine would be pressed on us, all sorts of unintelligible advice given with much drama, gesticulations and arm waving. The small communities would gather around staring in amazement at *'les fols Anglais'* before we were sent on our way with slaps on the back, handshakes and cries of *'Bon Voyage – Bon Courage!'*

Occasionally we would come across a bad hat, sometimes a surly and unfriendly lock-keeper who would not let us through but forced us to unload our boats and then watch as we carried everything to a point beyond his jurisdiction where we had to reload it all before setting off again.

On a couple of occasions a bargee, seemingly hell bent on our destruction, would bear down on us forcing our tiny craft to the very water's edge where we were grounded on rocks as the barge sucked the water from under us on its way past. Such is life; we would have found these characters anywhere but, in the main, the rural French community and canal folk were warm, generous and helpful. These ordinary country folk made us feel most welcome – something that has never been lost on me.

We pressed on to Digoin, our most southerly point on the Loire before turning north-east towards Montceau. Here the night temperature fell to well below freezing making life pretty uncomfortable first thing. By this stage most of our possessions were sodden and each morning we had to force our way back into our frozen canoeing clothes. A few hours in the boats soon warmed things up, in fact the afternoon sunshine made paddling the heavy laden boats hard and thirsty work. Montceau on the 17th followed by Chagny two days later – we had reached the Saone at last. Now, turning south, we pointed ourselves in the direction of our destination some 450 kilometres ahead.

The Saone is a beautiful river and October is a wonderful time to see this part of France where, in the next few days, we passed close to some of the great vineyards of the region, the vines ablaze in the last of their autumn colours. Seeing such an expanse of beautiful countryside from the river at our steady pace was another quite unforgettable experience. We breathed the fresh, cool autumn air, had time to take in the sights and sounds of the countryside and got a feeling for the great peace, beauty and the space of rural France – something that could never be done speeding along in a car. A few days of steady progress like this brought us to Lyon on the 23rd. Here we met the Rhone.

Lyon is huge and built at the point where the two big rivers join forces before rushing together down to the Mediterranean. Eventually, and with much help from the river authorities, we reached the great Rhone-Saone lock. Peering nervously over the edge we saw the Rhone in all its glory – not only the promised current but, because the water was low, large areas of rapids with long tracts of rocks and shoals.

Wherever the water ran fast and deep, mighty barges were forcing their way upstream against the current. It looked as though life from this point on might get interesting, and I wished that I was in something a little stronger than our dear old canoe that held all our worldly possessions in a thin wooden frame whose canvas now had patches on the patches.

Eventually the lock gates opened and we were away – in fact we shot out into the main stream. I have no idea how fast we were going but I

*'We passed close to some of the great vineyards of the region.'*

remembered seeing some boys running along the quay trying to keep up with us. We swept past them and out into the main current, their shouts falling away far behind. This was a whole new experience and the trick now was to remain afloat, to keep together and try to work out how to stop for the night. If one of us was to go over now we would indeed be at the mercy of our Maker.

We managed to pull into the shore, pitched camp and took stock of the situation. Time was running on so we decided to push our good luck to the very limit and just keep going. Next morning another new experience – a thick fog lay across the water and visibility fell to less than fifty yards as we were carried out into the gloom by the strong current.

After a short while we stopped rowing for out there, somewhere ahead of us, we could hear the ominous sound of rushing water. Unable to control events we were swept into a long stretch of vicious and turbulent rapids. On top of it all we could hear the horns of barges warning everybody and everything to get out of their way. Some hope of that! It was simply a question of hanging on and sometimes it pays not to have too vivid an imagination. That day we did almost 100 kilometres before lunch.

We had heard tales of the fearsome Mistral wind that roars down the Rhone valley pulling with it other winds from out of the surrounding hills and whipping the surface of the water into white horses. On the 27th we found ourselves just north of Avignon. The weather was foul and we packed up camp in a heavy drizzle and steadily rising wind. Sometime after nine the Mistral struck in all its glory – quite literally we got it right in the neck.

The sky blackened, the rain fell in torrents and we were pushed along helplessly in front of a huge wind that churned the surface of the river into steep waves. It was too much for the canoes and two of them began to sink. Struggling ashore through the waves we took cover from the elements as best we could, soaked to the skin, frozen and thoroughly rattled by the experience.

The next day was our last and the weather remained grim. Sheets of rain were falling and what appeared to be a full gale had blown flat the tall reeds along the canal bank. Breaking camp in such conditions was not much fun but we forced ourselves to get on with it and, shortly before midday, came to the small commercial harbour of Port du Bouc where the Etang was to be our final leg into Marseilles. Sadly, further progress was out of the question.

Waves two metres and more were breaking along the shore line and out beyond the harbour wall on the Etang itself the sea was just a mass of seething spray. Some local fisherman told us that this Mistral was a good one and could last for anything up to a week. That was it: we took our faithful little boats out of the water for the last time and organised ourselves for the return trip, getting back to Plymouth a couple of days later.

When I got back I was asked me if I had enjoyed my holiday at the Queen's expense. I told them it had been hard work but fun and admitted that I had learned a lot about myself and about life. But also I had found France. One or two instances apart, it was a beautiful and peaceful country, full of kind, cheerful people who had gone out of their way to help us. I was deeply impressed by all I had experienced and remained determined to return one day and continue to explore this fascinating and attractive land.

Shading his eyes from the sun Gerard looked across at me with a thoughtful expression on his face.

'Well,' he said slowly, 'you certainly know your France, and you saw it from the best possible angle, at a good time of the year too. When you went through Valence on the Rhone you would have passed close to my aunt. She has a small chateau there; a lovely place close to the great St Joseph and Hermitage wines.'

We sat in silence for a few moments, each lost in his own thoughts until Gerard spoke again. 'And what happened after that? You promised me the other day you would tell me a bit about your time in the Army. That must have been just about the start of it all?'

There were just the two of us so it seemed a good enough time to go over some of my adventures but I warned him that, apart from little bits here and there, it had been an ordinary sort of career. It was one in which I had made my way in much the same fashion as had all the others.

Soon after the canoeing adventure we were posted across to Northern Ireland. It was long before the present troubles and, on the surface anyway, Ulster was just another peaceful corner of the UK where regiments were sent to get on with their lives until such time as they were wanted for more interesting assignments.

However it soon became obvious, even to us youngsters, that something was not right. The root cause was not difficult to find for, off the beaten track, Catholic communities were living, quite literally, under the heel of the Protestant majority who were discriminating against them quite outrageously over housing, jobs, health, education and welfare. The vast majority of people on both sides were very friendly to us and went out of their way to make us feel welcome wherever we went, but there, just beneath the surface, deep discontent was fermenting and would surely break out in earnest one day.

The 1960s were difficult times for the British Army which was being despatched to numerous corners of the old Empire where trouble of one sort or another had broken out. British Guiana – now Guyana – a small colony on the northern tip of South America was riven with inter-racial strife and, as the one British regiment there was unable to cope, reinforcements were sent to help keep the peace. We arrived to find the land of sunshine, rum and calypso a very sorry place indeed. In a number of ways it was a situation similar to the one we had left. Here again were two factions – Indians and Negros – who had never got on and now, through racial rather than religious differences, were at each others' throats.

There were horrible scenes of violence where a small section of one community had been attacked by mobs armed with cane machettes. Murder in its most gory form and terrible mutilations were the order of the day as was the burning of homes and property, sometimes with the wretched occupants forced to remain inside.

On other occasions we would come across the victims of crude bomb attacks or were confronted with the battered remains of those who had been beaten and clubbed to death. We did what we could to keep the two groups apart while the politicians attempted to bring some sort of order to the place. However, we felt that, in the end, it would be up to the people themselves to learn to accept one another and get on with their lives. We could not do that for them.

At about this time I decided to volunteer for service with the British special forces. Gerard knew something of them, in particular those who were raised during the last war initially to operate behind the lines. I went on to explain how their operations were then enlarged into intelligence gathering and working with partisans.

Later, in occupied France, they worked closely with the French Maquis, often combining to carry out raids against the occupying forces. Even now, fifty years on, old men meet at reunions and hark back to those difficult days. Little mercy was shown to those who were captured. Invariably they would be tortured then either shot out of hand or deported to concentration camps. Terrible reprisals were taken against the villagers around whom the Maquis and the British forces operated. Even today memories of those times are deeply emotional for those who were there. The reunions are sad occasions but ones where the old warriors can renew their strong bonds of camaraderie and friendship.

After the War the unit was expanded and conducted operations in a number of theatres where the British Army was involved. Lately, they have developed counter-terrorist skills and have conducted several successful operations, most of which have been accompanied by a great deal of unwanted publicity.

The regiment took volunteers from within the Army and subjected them to a rigorous month-long selection course. Those who were successful – usually no more than 10 per cent or so – then underwent a period of specialist training before joining the unit. I managed to defeat the examiners, completed the training and joined one of the four operational squadrons. They had just returned from the jungles of Borneo and were already preparing to go out to Aden and the Radfan mountains. Here, for a number of years, they had been involved in a tough, bitter campaign against the mountain tribes.

The soldiering was hard. The Radfan tribesmen, like the Pathans in Afghanistan, were natural fighters, expert marksmen and had a wonderful eye for the ground. Once they got the upper hand they would press home their attacks ruthlessly – it was a campaign in which no prisoners were taken and we never left our wounded. And it was here, too, that I first saw combat at close range and quickly learned that the business of killing or being killed was, despite whatever Hollywood had to say about it, pretty nerve-wracking stuff, sometimes terrifying, exhausting and always very messy.

Serving alongside men such as these was a great experience but, as officers, we had to leave the unit after three years to continue our career in the Army. I returned to my regiment which, after several years in Germany, was posted to the sunshine island of Malta – no mountain tribesmen there! However, this was in 1969 when the troubles in Northern Ireland finally came to a head. As part of a huge reinforcement programme we were sent into Belfast – the capital city of the North. The two communities seemed incapable of living in harmony, a situation as bizarre as it was tragic.

Those of us who had been there earlier were amazed and saddened at the dramatic changes which had taken place in such a short time. Gone was the happiness and laughter, the faces of the people in the streets now bore a strained and pinched look as they hurried about their business. The police were everywhere in strength, soldiers were on the streets with rifles and there was a grim, unhappy atmosphere about the whole Province.

We remained there for about four months before returning to Malta and our families. However, the situation continued to deteriorate rapidly and, no sooner had we got back, than we were warned for a second tour of duty the following year – this time along the border with the Republic.

Operations in the rural areas were very different from those in the town and we had to learn quickly how to react to these new circumstances. Here the IRA operated from safe havens, either from the villages along the border or indeed from across the border itself. It was a difficult and dangerous business, the enemy were clever, they held all the cards and we lost a number of men.

Later, in 1973 when I was at the Army Staff College, I was recalled to the special forces, this time to command one of the squadrons. The war in Oman was then at its height and stability in the Middle East was in danger of collapsing. Communism had spread along the southern coast of Arabia and a determined effort was being made to overthrow the Sultan of Oman. Had this been successful the narrow Straits of Hormuz, through which much of the West's oil flows, would have been closed, with catastrophic results.

The small and ill-equipped Sultan's army had been unable to stem this advance and we were deployed into the mountains to counter further advances. Once again we found ourselves fighting a tough campaign against insurgents, a long way from home and with little support available – plus ça change!

I did two five-month operational tours in Oman whilst back with the old firm, and it was between the two of them that I returned to France and went down to Pau where I first saw the beautiful countryside of the south-west. After my second tour, I was posted to the British Army in Germany. It was the first time I had encountered armoured warfare, in fact I had never even been inside a tank or armoured personnel carrier – and have not been near one of the wretched things since.

The whole business was new to me and I found it all acutely uncomfortable, cumbersome and claustrophobic. And here too, so I was reliably informed, many a budding career was brought to a sticky end. I viewed it all with some trepidation and decided to tread warily.

Mercifully my General was new to this game as well. General Frank Kitson was one of the British Army's most radical brains. A clever and highly decorated soldier, he came as a breath of fresh air to a command where the training, thinking and attitudes had become hidebound and stereotyped.

A year later I was promoted and went off to NATO's Defence College in Rome before taking up my next appointment as the personal staff officer to a senior German Commander-in-Chief in southern Holland. If the HQ of a British Division is big, a major NATO HQ is simply enormous, added to which there are the customs, languages and military procedures to complicate matters. My tiny command post in the Oman mountains now seemed a very long way off – but how I longed to be there. The General for whom I was to work commanded all the Allied air and land forces between the Baltic and the Italian border. But there were no French – officially anyway.

Looking back it seems incredible that, while we all lined up in Germany to face the might of the Warsaw Pact, the French, whose country was just behind us, were not there playing the game. It all stemmed from those momentous decisions many years previously when de Gaulle removed France from the military alliance. However, although not there officially, we had a small and dedicated French military liaison team with us, and how they worked, trying to organise what we would all have to do to fit them in, come the day.

Whether or not our efforts would have been successful we will never know, but one fact was for certain. Throughout the year each nation threw an official party on its selected day. The day for France was, not surprisingly, Bastille Day and this was, without doubt, the party of the year when the French General and his small staff, together with their families, entertained us lavishly with the gastronomic delights and great wines of their country.

Early in 1981 I learned that I was to take command of my own regiment the following year. We were to be in England initially but were then due to move over to Northern Ireland for two years. I had mixed feelings. On one hand to get command of one's own regiment was a great honour and nothing could mean more to me than 'Going home' to the family regiment I had joined more than twenty years before. On the other hand the news about the tour of duty in Ireland disturbed me. There were eight to ten regiments there at any one time. Two or three of them would go for a short four-month tour. They went without families and, after a period of intensive training, went into the hard operational areas.

The remainder went accompanied by their families for a two-year tour. They were settled into the quieter areas and usually they did not have an operational area of their own – their soldiers being used as reinforcements for other units. This was fine for the junior officers and men but not much fun for the commander who would be without an operational command. Sadly, my worst fears were realised and I learned that my regiment was to be garrisoned on a lonely, windswept peninsular far removed from most of the action.

Life became frustrating and difficult. Things were not going well at home and, at around this time, my marriage broke down. For many years Thelma, my wife, had followed the drum faithfully, often having to bring up the boys on her own when I was away. Sometimes she had to move house by herself with all the attendant problems of reorganising the home and beginning a new social life for her and our sons. Such a life is not everybody's cup of tea and this tour proved to be one too many. We separated and I spent much of the remaining months on my own.

The final days were very sad. I had grown immensely fond and very proud of my regiment and, due to the peculiar circumstances I found myself in, had got to know many of the wives and families as well as all the six hundred or so men. It was like parting from one's own family and when on that last morning I bade farewell to my staff I must confess that there was a lump in my throat.

I walked across the parade ground to my landrover which, true to our tradition, was to be pulled out of the gates of the camp by my officers and sergeants, the route being lined by the men. My driver was waiting for me outside the camp gates and we drove slowly through the beautiful, sad countryside of Northern Ireland. When we reached the Belfast docks I bade L/Cpl Thorne a fond farewell and boarded the night ferry to leave the country for the last time.

The last few months had been a bit tough but, looking back over the years, I had had a great time in the Army. I had no regrets and would do it all over again if I was given the chance. Then, in 1987, I learned that I was to be promoted again and that my new job was to be at the School of Infantry.

'Well,' Gerard said slowly, 'You certainly got around a bit and did your fair share. It's not often I get to hear it all like that. It's very different from our system – your family regiments, the special forces and so forth. But you know, underneath it all there are tremendous similarities with most careers – it's a question of getting on with the job, having a touch of luck here and there, and getting the timing right.'

That was it in a nutshell, and we talked on for a while until the sound of engines signalled the return of the soldiers who were due to spend the afternoon shattering the peace and quiet of the place with their guns.

A week or so later I was invited over to sample the very best of French cuisine. Marie-Claire came from Bordeaux and never failed to produce a memorable supper. After the meal we sat chatting and eventually Gerard came to talk about his time at Pau, the home of the French Airborne School. He knew I had been there and knew also how I detested anything to do with parachuting.

There used to be two sorts of parachutists in the special forces: the free-fall troops who, quite literally, lived for parachuting and the rest of us. We loathed the very idea – cowards to a man – and treated the sanity of the others with the deepest suspicion. Mention the very word and the room would be emptied. Parachuting for the average soldier was an evil that had to be endured, something that our masters had decreed we had to do and that was that. Gerard laughed at this and admitted that many of his contemporaries felt the same way and were happy enough to leave the heroics to the lunatics and youngsters.

Needless to say I was amongst the very worst of the parachutists and one day, whilst on a training jump, I landed badly breaking my right leg. Later in the year we exercised in France where we were to be dropped into an area just to the north of the Pyrenees and then move through the countryside whilst being hunted by Gerard's old regiment and their friends from the Foreign Legion.

I was sent on ahead to Pau to help organise the exercise and here I came across the breathtaking scenery of the south-west. The Pyrenees are a majestic sight at any time of the year but now, in the autumn, the high peaks had their first covering of snow and were an awesome spectacle. To the north of the mountains the land fell gently away in undulating waves of wooded hills and long deep valleys towards the plains of Gascony and Languedoc.

There was an aura of space and peace about the countryside, just as I remembered from my earlier visit. The roads were empty save for the farm traffic and the country folk going about their business. The small towns and villages seemed almost to be in a time warp as if I was looking at a community from a byegone age. I was enthralled by it all and, once again, felt determined to come back yet again and explore the countryside at a more leisurely pace and to study its history.

Gerard had been based down there a number of times and knew this corner of France well. He and Marie-Claire went over the maps telling me about the countryside and the people of the south-west, of the great wines and the food produced down there and a little about the long and often bloody history.

'Did you realise,' Gerard asked, 'that the last place the British fought the French in France was down at Toulouse, a year before Waterloo?'

'Yes,' I replied, 'my regiment was there and we gave you a good hiding then too, didn't we?'

'Rubbish, it was a draw,' he shouted with a big grin. 'And in any case we only had our second XV on the field – Napoleon was on leave at the time!'

Netheravon was a happy place where everyone worked together to achieve the best possible results. Later, as news of the Gulf War filtered back, we were gratified to hear that our efforts at pushing the students as hard as we could on realistic training had paid off.

It was a good way to finish and Netheravon was my last command. A number of things were happening in my life that prompted me to have a serious look at what lay out there beyond the Army. I was becoming restless and felt that it was perhaps time for a complete change of scenery.

# CHAPTER II

# *Beginnings*

For some time I had been toying with the idea of buying my own
house and getting away from Aldershot. Whatever the future might
hold I would have to find my own home, for the Army did not take
kindly to officers squatting illegally in their married quarters once they
had left the system. Hugo, my elder son, who had been working in
Winchester, loved it there, and had often told me about the city. It is
one of the most beautiful cities in England, the ancient capital before
London where many of the Saxon kings lay buried. The magnificent
Norman cathedral towers over the city and inside lies King William II,
son of the Conqueror from Normandy.

If I was really serious about this idea, he urged, then I should come
down and have a look. It lies further to the west than Aldershot, closer
to my family home in Devon and to where Jamie, my younger lad, was
then still at school. I decided to take the plunge and bought a small
house on the outskirts of the city a short while after taking up my job at
Netheravon. No sooner had I settled than Gerard and Marie-Claire
came out to see where I was living. We walked around Winchester and
they both remarked that it bore a strong resemblance to Auch, a lovely
old city, an hour to the west of Toulouse in south-west France.

Soon after the move to Winchester a very important little fellow came
into my life. Some good friends living nearby had been breeding Jack

Russells and one day they called and asked me over for a drink. I was greeted at the front door by the usual yapping, tumbling mass of Jacks but in addition, behind them, four very little people were waddling their way towards me. Not in the least bit afraid, their tails up and wagging, they came up to my shoes, inspected them closely and agreed to let me pass.

It was, of course, a set-up job. Gay and David Nevil, realising that I was on my own again, reckoned I needed company. Polly, their little bitch had whelped some four weeks previously and I was introduced to the one remaining ownerless member of the litter. Sat firmly in a deep armchair, a large glass of whisky pressed into my hand, Patch was placed in my lap. The room fell silent as we studied one another in some detail before he tucked himself up into a little ball and fell asleep. That was it: two weeks later I returned and picked up this little scrap of perpetual motion and he has been with me ever since.

We were inseparable and in those early days Patch would curl up inside my beret on the seat beside me as we drove to work. He came everywhere and was particularly fond of the wild open countryside of Salisbury Plain where the Army had their ranges. Totally unaffected by the crash of gunfire he would wander out in front of the machine-guns as they were firing and hunt for rabbits and mice in the grass as torrents of metal flew just a few inches above his head. Occasionally he would put up a hare which would lope gently away with Patch in pursuit, yelping with excitement, his little legs galloping away to the shouts of encouragement from the soldiers.

He was my confidant, my bedside companion and walking partner as well as being a great friend who never told tales out of school. Now, all these years later, he is in the evening of his life and were he able to look back over the last eleven years he could tell many a story about how our lifestyle began to change soon after we met.

I was beginning to meet a number of people in Winchester about this time, many of whom were associated with the cathedral and the appeal that had been launched to raise money for the restoration of the great church. I often used to take myself off to Evensong and sit behind the choir entranced by the wonderful singing. The cathedral choir was well known the world over and had produced numerous tapes and discs, however there was something special about them when they sang at home. Sometimes they would sing anthems composed by my ancestor, Sir Hubert Parry, and I always found these occasions deeply moving. In addition to the choir there was a most impressive lay choral society – the Wayneflete Singers – who would join up with the choir to perform major works accompanied by a symphony orchestra, always beautifully sung and always to a full audience.

I got to know a number of members due to the fact that The Wykeham Arms, a very old and famous Winchester watering hole, lay just beyond King's Gate outside the cathedral grounds and, after rehearsals, they used to gather there for a drink. I enjoyed the occasional evening at The Wykeham and would sometimes take my house guests there for dinner. One evening, whilst I was talking to a group of friends, introductions were made, amongst them to one of the singers.

She was tall and quiet with a soft voice and a gentle way about her. We did not say much to each other there and then but next time we met we got talking. Her name was Rachel. She lived a few miles the other side of Winchester in a pretty little village called Itchen Stoke and we agreed to meet again to walk the dog – well done Patch! Two years later we got married but in between times we planned our great adventure that was to take us away from all that we knew in England to a new home and life in south-west France.

Rachel, although born in Derbyshire, had strong Irish connections – her father coming from the south, and her mother being part Irish. Her father had become a member of the Church and this had entailed the family moving around the country from time to time. Years before they had planned to take up a life as missionaries in Africa but her father's poor health had prevented this. In 1960 when Rachel was eight they moved to Scotland then, five years later, came south again to London. Here she continued her education in one of the city's exclusive Grammar

Schools which she loved, excelling at English, French and, in particular, music as she played both piano and cello.

Whilst still at school she was offered a place at the Royal Academy of Music to further her studies but decided instead to spend a year in France away from it all. On returning home she again put off her entrance to the Royal Academy, preferring to seek work in London. In 1974 she was married but, sadly, it did not last and in 1980 she found herself on her own with her two young sons.

Times were hard and she took up the piano once more, gaining her teaching diploma before moving close to Winchester where she lived in a little thatched cottage beside the river Itchen. She began to teach privately becoming immersed in the musical life of the city and cathedral where she joined the choral society. It was here, after one of the evening rehearsals, that we were introduced to each other.

I had been thinking about France as well as a number of other possibilities for some time before we met. The idea of packing up everything and leaving home was certainly an exciting idea as my visits to France over the years had shown. However, there were many important decisions that had to be made and an awful lot of soul searching to be done if it was to be got right. Rachel was no stranger to France, in fact she knew far more about the country and the people than me. She had first been there as a young girl of just thirteen when she was sent on an exchange visit to a farming family in a small village near Nantes.

After this visit her parents played hosts to a succession of young French girls who came over to England with a student organisation. She loved the culture and way of life in France and returned later, this time as an au pair to a well-to-do family who lived in Versailles.

She accompanied the family to their summer villa at Le Cap Ferrat on the Bassin d'Arcachon where they spent their time sailing dinghies in the great Bassin or playing in the surf, amongst the wonderful sand dunes and along the golden beaches. Here, so she would tell me with a wistful smile, she first fell madly and beautifully in love with a devastating young Frenchman. The curtains were, however, kept tightly drawn and I never got to learn more about young Claude and his affaire d'amour with the tall, shy Irish girl whose long dark hair and large hazel eyes had stolen his heart.

Occasional trips were made to another family home down in the Pays Basque country at Hendaye close to the Spanish border. Here she would wander slowly through the wonderful markets in Irun chatting to the stall owners or play in the hills that came down to the sea, with the youngsters in her care.

Later she was to travel to Paris and the Dordogne where she spent holidays with her young sons, and then, a short while before I met her she had been to the Haute Savoie where she and some friends would go walking in the high Alps during the summer months. Here she met up with a ski instructor and his wife – Jean Claude and Sylvie – who showed her the mountains that were now silent and empty, the host of noisy skiers having gone on their way. She saw the wildlife and flowers that abound in that beautiful part of France once the snows have receded to the high mountain peaks.

She developed a great affection for the French, she admired their way of life and she spoke the language well – her friends joked that, one day, she would surely go there to live. As we got to know one another we realised that we were both at something of a crossroads in our lives. She had been on her own for some time after her marriage had failed and was living with her younger son who was at school nearby. An accomplished musician, she had taken up teaching the piano to help pay the bills and, whilst enjoying her job, she did not relish spending the rest of her days doing just that. She too was becoming restless.

I was still a soldier and working away quite happily at Netheravon although my papers were now in and my card would have been marked. If successful, I would soon be leaving after I had finished my present job. France, whilst indeed a romantic dream, was a long way off and the idea might well come to naught. If I was going to leave then I had better start looking around for a second career. Interesting jobs were hard to come by, well-paid ones scarcer still. For weeks I scanned the columns looking for something that stirred the imagination but nothing seemed to fit and I began to wonder if I could ever settle into another large organisation.

In the end I sent off just three application forms. Each one seemed to do the trick and got me an interview after which I received offers from those concerned. The first was for the post of British Club Manager to an exotic brand of foreign motorcar. I drove up to the Midlands and met them at their annual general meeting. Shortly afterwards I applied for another, this time it was for the post of General Manager to one of the great Hampshire country houses. Both interviews went well but I declined the subsequent offers. The more I looked at what I would be doing the more I realised that I would not have been particularly happy in either environment. I could not see myself in either job.

I was beginning to feel fairly confident that I would be able to find myself something but was becoming a little bit disenchanted with it all. Both jobs thus far consisted of the sort of dull, routine work that I had been doing in the Army years ago. Furthermore I would be doing it for less pay, for people I did not know and who, in the main, were far younger than me. Was that really the sort of thing I wanted? I decided to give it all one more go and then think again. I read that the Lord Mayor of London was looking for a Sword Bearer. The applicant was to have had a successful career to date, probably within the armed services, and should be a competent horseman.

I applied, and was told that they had received more than enough applications and that was that. Then, a few weeks later, I was asked to go to the office of the Lord Mayor in the City for an interview as most of those interviewed up to now had been unable to remain in the saddle when they had gone along for their equestrian test. I should point out that the appointment was, in effect, to be a member of the Lord Mayor's personal office staff – the Sword Bearing and riding bit was to do with the occasional ceremonial parades such as the Lord Mayor's show.

Nevertheless it would not look very good if the smart chap on the horse at the head of the procession kept falling off his horse in front of the TV cameras and all the tourists.

Whilst I had not ridden for some time I had been a member of the Army Modern Pentathlon team and had ridden to hounds for many years in my younger days. I reckoned that with a bit of luck I could probably remain attached to the animal but, now thoroughly suspicious of army officers' horsemanship, the selection committee invited me along to prove myself. One of the interview team lived in Surrey where he and his wife kept a number of horses.

The weekend before the London interview I drove across to Farnham and duly reported myself at the front door of this lovely country house. After climbing into my riding clothes and boots I was introduced to Harvey, a large, handsome bay gelding who was to be my mount for the next half hour or so. We looked at each other closely for a while when Harvey, having sniffed and blown inquisitively, began to nibble my jacket and push his head against me. He seemed happy enough with what was in front of him and, confident that we would get on together, I climbed aboard.

It was a nice little ride that took in a short course around their land, the owner's wife watching to see if I would follow my predecessors into the ditch. Both Harvey and I were beginning to enjoy ourselves doing the usual figures of eight, changing legs and so on before we were brought to a halt. There were a few jumps in the field and I asked my hostess if she would like to see what we could do with them.

'Oh no,' she laughed, 'That's not necessary. I just wanted to see if you knew what you were doing. If you found yourself leaping over things in the middle of London something would have gone very badly wrong!'

Harvey and I parted company and I prepared myself for the other half of my examination the following week. This was to be a formidable test. Not only did the interview panel consist of three ex-Lord Mayors plus a retired Admiral who was the secretary to the present incumbent, but I was to sample the delights of commuting from my home to the place of work and then back again in the evening. If I was going to find work in England then commuting would become part of my life and I had better get used to the idea.

I cannot remember exactly when I went up for the interview but it was sometime in the late spring. Winchester was looking at its best – the wisteria around King's Gate was in profusion and the swallows and swifts were wheeling around above the city having just returned from their winter holiday in Africa. I had been asked to appear in the morning so I decided to travel up early and have a look around the famous streets paved with gold. This meant that I would be swept along with the last of the rush hour.

It was years since I had travelled by train and my first taste of what was to come were the scenes I encountered at the station early that morning. Everywhere grim-faced, dark-suited men were pushing and shoving their way around the ticket office, forcing themselves urgently through the queue and around those at the paper stand, or past the wretched chap on the gate who was trying to check everyone's ticket. Hard-bitten, impatient women were in there battling away with the best of them; there was not much of the fair and gentle sex in evidence that morning.

When the 8.15 appeared the place erupted as everybody pressed forward in a most undignified manner, fighting their way on board in a desperate attempt to find a seat. I scrummaged down with the pack, managed to squeeze into a horribly overcrowded compartment and sat down. I could not move – caught in a vice-like grip between two men, one staring stonily ahead clasping his briefcase, the other wrestling with his newspaper. The train jerked into motion and we rumbled on our way, everybody in acute discomfort and sitting in an unreal, funereal silence.

I was feeling wretchedly uncomfortable by this stage but I had yet to experience the underground line known quaintly as 'The Drain'. I waited patiently until the train had emptied, alighted cautiously and was promptly caught up in the hordes just disgorged from other trains. This great mass of humanity half walked, half ran towards the ticket barrier, everyone looking worried, anxious and thoroughly unhappy with their lot. Here at the gate I paused momentarily to ask the way, blocking the exit in the process, causing everyone around me to trip and tangle with each other, cursing me roundly in the process. By now I was convinced that the whole world had gone barking mad.

The main underground ticket office at Waterloo is no place to stop for a chat during the rush hour. To do so is akin to pulling up in the fast lane of a busy motorway when those around tend to get excited. I did not know my way nor the cost of my fare so I asked. The person within, mercifully screened from view by the filthy plastic grill, snapped back at me and I was despatched down a long, dark corridor from which came the constant rumbling of the trains and a hot wind.

On board I experienced what I believe is known as flesh pressing. Quite simply everybody was forced up against one another, any attempt at modesty, decency or courtesy abandoned. I found myself face to face with a sour-looking female who stared at some point in space behind me. Whilst intimate body contact from top to toe was unavoidable I sensed she was waiting for some demonstration of my predatory instincts when she would raise cane.

No such luck, I could not have moved even if I had fancied closer contact with this hideous sexless creature. Nasty, squidgy things were being pressed up against me from behind, I was hemmed in by sweating bodies of all shapes and sizes. The smell was appalling, garlic suppers, halitosis and broken wind all heaped together in some awful malodour.

Mercifully, the nightmare was short lived and I got up to the street again where I paused to regain my composure, tidy myself up and take stock. I had shut the front door to my house more than two hours earlier. That meant almost five hours of this madness each and every day, twenty-five hours each week or more than four days of my life each month. I could never take that, never.

I entered the great building quite calmly, the forthcoming interview now holding no fears for me as I had decided that I could not possibly live like this. In an almost light-hearted mood I was ushered into a long impressive room at the far end of which was a table and behind this sat the four men who were to interview me. All were quite charming, put me at my ease and, after introducing themselves, proceeded to grill me expertly and thoroughly about absolutely everything.

The interview lasted for over an hour and 1 suppose I should have felt drained at the end of it but, rather to the contrary, I found it a stimulating and most enjoyable experience. Lord Mayors of London are always impressive men who have risen up through the ranks of the City. Here were three of them, all most courteous, witty and very clever. Each had been outstandingly successful in their chosen professions and I knew them all as well-known public figures.

The interview over I retraced my steps to Winchester. The ghastly crowds had gone – Heaven knows where to or what they were now all doing – and the train seemed a haven of peace and calm. The sun was well up and shining brightly into the carriage. I felt hot and uncomfortable. I longed to get out and shuddered at the thought of ever having to repeat the morning's experiences. That was to be that and when I was rung the following day I could do none other than decline their kind offer.

Rachel understood that I was not cut out for that sort of life and for some days we talked at length about the various options open to us and where we should go from here. The three interviews had shown me that I was unlikely to be happy working for anybody else, perhaps I could manage part-time or freelance work but no longer as a small cog in a big machine. For more than thirty years I had been a member of a large organisation, doing what I was bidden and I felt the time had come to try something on my own.

The more we tried to steer our way around the subject of France the more it featured in our minds until one evening over dinner we decided to stop kicking against it and to examine the possibilities instead. It was a huge subject with all sorts of factors to consider and problems to be worried through and we were determined to study every angle before getting carried away with the idea. However the very thought of what might lie ahead filled us with excitement and a sense of adventure. We were, so we felt, looking at something quite different. Was there, perhaps, a new life for us together out there after the years we had spent on our own? France now became the focus of our attention.

# CHAPTER III

# Decisions, Decisions

*France – studying the problem. What were we going to do? And where?*
*The essential requirements. We settle for Toulouse. French rural property.*

We sat down and asked ourselves what, if we really wanted to go to France, was going to be the point of it all? What were we going to do? From the start it was obvious that we were going to have to work for our living and could not just disappear into thin air. Her Majesty was not exactly generous with her pension schemes and we needed the extra money to live, added to which, if we went out and did nothing – took very early retirement – we would drive each other up the wall. Both of us were energetic and needed a challenge.

What sort of work? For a variety of reasons we both felt that it would have to be in the holiday business, catering principally for the English-speaking market. There were enough people doing this already for us to find out what sort of income we might expect from our efforts and perhaps, if we proceeded cautiously, we could learn from others. For the moment anyway we would concentrate our minds on this and not allow ourselves to become distracted. Unless we came up against something that forced us to change, all our planning and preparation would go towards this.

We felt that we should not become involved in any form of leisure or activity holidays such as sailing, mountain walking, skiing or whatever. It would only complicate matters. Something like that might be developed later but in the early days our energies and resources would be fully occupied in getting the home set up. People could come and stay with us and then go off for the day to do their own thing. To attempt anything more at this stage would be courting disaster. We would keep it all as simple as possible.

There appeared to be four options within this particular scenario – the caravan and camping scene, *gîtes*, B&B or a small hotel. We did not spend too much time thinking about the caravan and camping scene. We both found the idea of being surrounded by caravans or mobile homes, ablution blocks, netball courts, together with hordes of screaming children too dreadful for words.

The idea of a small hotel had its appeal but there seemed to be too many imponderables. How small was small – eight rooms, twelve rooms or what? And what about running it all – the staff, employment laws, health and safety regulations, social benefit and all that? We had heard that employing people could be something of a minefield and fought shy of this idea.

*Gîtes* and B&B sounded fairly straightforward and, as these were popular activities, we should be able to find out a bit more about it without too much trouble. It was difficult to determine which of these two options would be easier or the more profitable so, in the end, we decided to hedge our bets and try to do a bit of both if we could find the right place – the one complementing the other. We would begin by looking for a decent-sized house with some outbuildings that would suit our needs.

There are wonderful properties of all shapes and sizes throughout France. From Calais to Cannes, Bordeaux to Besancon the *immobiliers'* windows are crammed full of mouth-watering properties, all of which appear to be so much cheaper and more exciting than similar properties in the UK.

This brought us on to another very important point which we had to clarify before we got too excited by bricks and mortar. Exactly where did we want to do this? It would be quite hopeless to have a nice home in an unsuitable corner of France. Every part of rural France has its own particular charm and people choose different areas for different reasons.

Some prefer the north-west – the Breton coast – which is where our friends Roz and Graham Jefferies have their home and holiday business. Others choose to live and work in the Alps or Provence while others settle in the Dordogne. We had to decide where we wanted to be before we went across and started looking for a house. France is a huge place and it would be a grave error to go over there and wander aimlessly around the countryside like a child in a sweet shop.

In order to help us decide on the location, size and shape of our new home we decided to draw up a short list of imperatives – sine quae non – and force ourselves to stick to them. The first imperative for us was to be as warm as possible. We did not want to end up burned to a crisp like those who live in southern Spain but we wanted a decent climate where the summers would be long and the winters mild.

This immediately ruled out four-fifths of France and we found ourselves looking at the area south of a line between Bordeaux and Nice. Anything north of this, we decided, would be too cold. However, if we were going to be south of this line, we would be a long way from the UK – our principal market, as well as our family and friends.

This meant that we had to be near a major communication centre combining an international airport, motorways and the TGV. We could not expect our guests to fly in, pick up their car then drive for hours, map-reading their way across France like long-distance rally drivers. This then became our second imperative and to the south of our line there are four such centres: Nice, Marseilles, Toulouse and Bordeaux. We decided to ring each airport with a 45-minute driving circle and have a look at what went on inside each one. It soon became obvious that all four areas were very different – as was the cost of living – and this meant the value of property.

Within our 45-minute circle of the airports we had to be close to a decent-sized town. This was to be our third imperative: it would be no good at all if we had to set out on a long drive every time we wanted a loaf of bread. We needed to be near a town where there were supermarkets, doctors, dentists, chemists, hairdressers, DIY centres and, above all else, a good school. If all this was to come to pass then Tristan, Rachel's younger son, would be coming with us and his schooling still had some distance to run, thus we had to be close to a good-sized town.

The fourth point was that the property had to be in pretty fair condition. We were quite prepared to do a number of things to the place but I had no desire to spend our first winter camping in the garden while a new roof was put on. It would be a very direct route to another divorce. Fifth, the property had to be in an attractive setting and the sixth and last point was that we were after a place that had an air of dignity and elegance about it.

As a footnote we stressed to all the agents we contacted that we planned to come out and have a look when some likely places had been unearthed and we would not be amused to find ourselves conned into looking at rubbish. We did not want any horrors such as a line of pylons running past the front door or a pig farm at the bottom of the garden. The actual site of the property had to be good. We were asking a lot but we had given ourselves plenty of time.

For days we scoured the property columns of the papers noting the details of the agents working in our most likely areas of interest. It was hit and miss stuff but one day we came across an advertisement for a paper called the *French Property News*.

It was exactly what we wanted and contained more relevant information about the property scene in France than we had dared hope. Not only were there adverts for properties of every kind but many people who were involved with property, either directly or obliquely, were advertising their services or writing articles. We studied several copies and saw that they ran a number of exhibitions, one of which was due to open shortly.

The French Property Exhibition in Hammersmith turned out to be more of a property fair than an exhibition. Numerous *immobiliers* had their stands but, in addition, many others were there who were involved with property such as builders, architects and landscape gardeners. It was exactly what we needed and I have advised many who are considering a move to France to take out a subscription for the paper, go to some of the exhibitions and talk to those who are involved. Of course there is a certain amount of sales pressure but, as long as the homework has been done, much useful information can be gleaned and muddled ideas clarified.

We returned from our visit with the briefcase full of leaflets, details of properties and copious notes. After talking to a number of *immobiliers* and discussing our plans we left our address with those whose ideas we liked and who were operating in the area we had selected.

The following six months or so saw some 750 sets of details pouring through our letterbox. There was something for everyone from enormous, imposing chateaux perched loftily on some distant Pyrenean mountainside to tumbledown ruins surrounded by woods and brambles. We waded through everything, put most of them in the bin but ended up with about 50 that were roughly the size and shape we were looking for. Gradually we were beginning to zero in on our future home but there was a long way to go.

At this point we had to bid farewell to the Nice option. The prices in this smart corner of France were beyond our means and although there were a few that might have been within range, the locations went against them. One or two others were suspiciously cheap and there is always a very good reason for a property to be underpriced. We were not prepared to go all the way down there and have our suspicions confirmed.

There was not much between the value of properties in the other three areas so we set about examining each locality. Some time before I met Rachel, while the idea of a home in France was still in its infancy, I had taken a short trip to the area around the western corner of the Mediterranean between Beziers and Toulouse. A great friend of mine who was with me in the Army came too. Tony had some ideas about what he might like to do in this area and we spent some time looking closely at the country. The coastal region, while attractive in many places, does not immediately catch the eye and inland from the coast there is an area of flat plain that is often rather dull and featureless.

We did not go as far as Marseilles on this occasion but a study of the map revealed that the area around the airport would be unlikely to attract the sort of clients we would be seeking. Furthermore this was the Mediterranean coast and we had no plans to get tied up with that sort of holiday business. Whilst millions flock to the beaches with their children clasping buckets and spades we would be setting out to attract clients who had other things in mind. After some deliberation we decided to drop the Marseilles option. We were now left with two areas: Toulouse and Bordeaux.

The airport at Bordeaux is to the west of the city – as indeed it is at Toulouse – thus our 45-minute driving circle from the airport would be rather lopsided around the city. To the north-west of Bordeaux lies one of the great wine-growing areas of the world and this was not for us. Property here tended to be expensive and, except for the more serious wine buffs, the countryside would be of little interest to the average client.

To the west of the city, the south-west and south-east the land was flat and pine clad. We felt that this area, known as Les Landes, would not suit our needs either. This left the eastern quadrant and we gave this area a bit of thought. The land was indeed beautiful but in one area there was a preponderance of vineyards and to the north of this lay the Dordogne.

The valley of the Dordogne is renowned not only for its beauty but for the size of the British community that has chosen to settle there. Whilst we had nothing whatsoever against our fellow countrymen we were not going to go to all this trouble just to end up in an area boasting village cricket and bridge clubs and find ourselves in a part of the country that would, throughout the holiday season, be swamped by a mass of British holidaymakers. In addition, the further one went up the valley of the Dordogne, the longer it was going to take to get to and from the airport. We looked hard at the countryside around Bordeaux and, whilst there were indeed possibilities here, we decided to turn our attention instead to the area around Toulouse.

The more we studied this area the more it fascinated us. The countryside was superb – to the south lay the magnificent Pyrenees, to the west the Gers, renowned for its beauty, its gastronomic delights and for one of the Three Musketeers. The beauty of the area had captivated me when I was stationed at Pau in the foothills of the Pyrenees.

To the north and north-east was the valley of the Tarn, a beautiful river along which were many historic towns and cities including Albi and the vineyards of Gaillac. To the east were the Black Mountains of Languedoc, the Corbieres, Carcassonne and the Mediterranean – not Golf de St Tropez to be sure but the Med nonetheless. Finally the border with Spain was just a short drive to the south.

Then Toulouse itself caught our attention. A city of great historic and cultural interest it is also one of France's great centres of education where there are now three universities boasting more than 100,000 students between them. Known as *La Ville Rose* on account of the soft, pink hue of the brick that makes up so many of the buildings, Toulouse is indeed beautiful. Numerous attractive *places* and public gardens lie throughout the city while, in the very centre – Place du Capitole – is the magnificent Hotel de Ville and the opera house.

A further point that attracted us was that France had decided to make Toulouse, on account of its location, the high-tech centre of southern Europe and for some time had been pouring billions of francs into the infrastructure of the region. Toulouse, already alive and kicking, was booming rather than suffering a lingering death like so many great European cities. This, we felt, would bring all sorts of advantages to our venture.

Toulouse and its environs thus became the centre of our attention and we determined to redouble our efforts in finding out more about the area until either our mind was made up or we came across some horror that put us off. I returned to our 45-minute circle around the airport and looked for sizeable towns within this area. There were about six, only three of which boasted a good *lycée* and, after running a ten-minute driving circle around these three towns the area of search for our new home in France became small and manageable.

It was within these three small areas that we decided to concentrate our efforts. Through the good offices of the *French Property News*, the magazine *France* and Sunday papers we found a number of agents who dealt with this area in particular and pressed them for further details of properties with our specifications. Again we were bombarded with a mass of paper most of which followed their predecessors straight into the bin, but out of them all there were several that caught the eye, a number were within our selected areas and, of these, a few that appeared to be within our budget.

One point in the study stood out and caused me to think carefully – the price of property in this part of rural France seemed to be so much cheaper than elsewhere in Europe. There appeared to be no simple answer and, for certain, it was not a matter of supply and demand. Considering that France is one of the world's great playgrounds with almost seventy million visitors each year, it is difficult to understand why property is not actually more expensive here rather than less so. I was a bit suspicious about this and set about finding the answer.

One principal reason for this strange situation is that the average French rural homeowner does not have either the desire or the means to maintain his property in a presentable and desirable condition. Quite simply there was not, even a few years ago, the money available in rural France to carry out the maintenance. A glance at any house of some age in the country, any farm and most chateaux reveals that a great many are in dire need of repair and modernisation. Access to the place is often difficult and what passes for the garden or *parc* and the outbuildings frequently leave much to be desired.

Until recently, houses, even those close to the large cities, could be found without a vestige of sanitation, no form of heating other than the open hearth, just a cold tap in the kitchen and roofs that gaily channelled the water into the houses and onto the occupants. The owners had, for whatever reason, simply let the place go and the cost of restoration was prohibitive. It is impossible to imagine a situation such as this in an attractive part of rural England such as the countryside around Oxford, Salisbury or Guildford.

Another point is that French rural life tends to be far more parochial than country life elsewhere. Until the recent exodus from the countryside rural communities were more or less static. Property tended to get handed down through the family rather than being sold on to an outsider, the young staying on and helping run the family home or farm rather than seeking employment elsewhere. As no outside money came into these rural areas, property rarely changed hands and there was little or no turnover.

The very large and static rural population had to be housed somewhere and, once the exodus got underway, most chose to try their luck in the towns and cities. Many thousands of dwellings were left deserted or with just a few inhabitants who could no longer keep the place together and who were eager to move on themselves. Thus, when outsiders did come into the area there was an enormous choice available. A buyer would have been able to pick and choose before driving a hard and often cruel bargain, the vendors being desperate to sell.

An additional factor was the sheer size of the countryside in which all these properties lay. Modern amenities and services did not reach into the far corners of the more remote areas until recently, the inhabitants leading a hardy but somewhat primitive lifestyle. It was easy enough to pick up a cheap cottage or farm tucked away in the beautiful countryside but not so easy to bring in the services essential for a civilised existence. This tended to make the purchaser offer an even lower price for what already seemed to be a most attractively priced property.

*'Just a few inhabitants who could no longer keep the place.'*

40

The exodus from the land began at much the same time in the UK as it did in France, but the great difference was that empty properties in England were bought almost immediately and modernised, while in France they often lay empty and neglected for years. The race to pick up bargains in the English countryside began in the immediate post-war years.

By the early 1960s the best of the bargains had gone and within a few years anything of value was hard to find. So great was the demand that by the 1970s barns and outhouses were being sold for development as were orchards and small plots of land at the bottom of the garden. But in France the vacated properties were left empty in their thousands and the differences in prices between the two countries widened dramatically.

Once given a bit of thought the situation was easy enough to understand and our suspicions about the value of properties in south-west France were largely dispelled. At this point Rachel decided that we should go out and have a look at the area. She had not been to that part of France and, although she liked the look of what she saw, she needed to be convinced before we went any further.

We went to another French Property Exhibition in London and met a number of the *immobiliers* who were dealing with the area around Toulouse. In particular we spent some time talking to a young freelance *immobilier* called Jonathan Carson. He agreed that the time had now come for a visit and that since he lived and worked in Toulouse we might like to consider his offer of help. We did and, just before Christmas 1991, we flew out to *La Ville Rose* to see for ourselves.

We had been studying the matter of a move for more than a year. By now we knew exactly what we wanted to do, where we wanted to begin our search and what we were looking for. The aim of our forthcoming visit was to confirm in our minds that the area around Toulouse was the most suitable for our needs. We were going to look at properties but, at this stage, had no plans to settle for one.

# CHAPTER IV

# The Search in France – and Success

*Our Search. Christmas in Toulouse. We find Bosc Lebat. Will it work? Life speeds up. Married. To France again – this time to sign.*

Two hundred and fifty miles south of Paris the Air France Captain began his long descent into Blagnac airport just to the west of Toulouse. It was a clear winter's afternoon and far below us we could see woodsmoke drifting gently from the chimneys of the houses dotting the countryside along the Garonne valley. Descending further we could now make out Toulouse beneath us. *La Ville Rose*, bathed in the afternoon sun, looked just as its name suggested.

Both the centre of the great city and the suburbs seemed to be built almost entirely of the famous pink brick with their Roman-style tiled roofs. Everywhere, between the houses, were tiny blue rectangles of swimming pools, now emptied for the winter but a reminder of the long, warm summers.

Rachel nudged me and nodded towards the window. 'Just look at that,' she gasped. 'What a fantastic sight!'

There, in the middle distance were the Pyrenees. Their lower slopes were wreathed in mist but the long line of snow-clad peaks stood out clearly, the high western slopes bathed in the afternoon sunlight. It was indeed a remarkable sight. As far as mountains go the Pyrenees are not all that high, rising to something over 11,000 feet at their highest points.

What is so impressive however is that this long line of high peaks stretches out as one of the world's great natural barriers between two countries – France and Spain. From Perpignan on the Mediterranean coast to St Jean de Luz on the Atlantic it is a barrier that has frustrated armies throughout history. As Gerard Lemain had joked, the British Army had fought the French here in 1814 after Wellington's army had struggled, with enormous difficulties, through this range of mountains.

We were soon down and into the spacious modern airport where we collected our baggage, picked up the hire car and set off with high hopes. We were going to decide first if we would be comfortable with this part of France and secondly if it was an area to which guests would wish to come for a holiday. We planned on spending the first few days looking at the west and south of Toulouse before moving into the city itself for Christmas.

The remaining few days were going to be spent driving around the east and north of the city. We had arranged to meet Jonathan, the *immobilier*, the following morning. He had a few properties in the area that he thought we might like to see and was planning to join us for part of our drive around. We would be looking at any houses he had on his books simply to get some idea of what our money could buy.

Our destination was the city of Auch about an hour's drive due west of Toulouse. It is the capital of the Gers department, a pretty place of some 25,000 people. It was certainly large enough for our require-ments, had excellent schools and everything else that we needed but, and it was a big 'but', it was right at the limit of our driving circle from Toulouse. This meant that we had to force ourselves to ignore anything further west, north or south of the town. We had heard that the countryside there was very beautiful but we had to steel ourselves to ignore it.

This is a great danger when looking at the countryside in France. Every hilltop and crest opens up a new vista, the countryside lying ahead is seemingly even more beautiful than that just passed through. Unless care is taken, those studying the countryside get pulled along by the sheer magic of it all, finishing up miles away from the area intended to be searched. In fact we did go for a quick look and, attractive though it was, we felt that it was just too remote for our requirements.

We met Jonathan as planned and he lead us off to the first house which turned out to be a veritable ruin. We banged on the front door and an old, gum-booted peasant appeared from the depths of the place muttering away to himself, surrounded by dogs, chickens and ducks.

The ancient building was in terminal decline and as we climbed the stairs and looked up at the great gaps in the ceiling plaster we knew that it would cost a fortune to put right. One look at the kitchen convinced Rachel that it was a non-starter. We left the poor old fellow standing in the rain as bemused and disappointed as vendors the world over when punters turn their backs and go on their way.

The next place was massive – and shut – the owner having decided that he had better things to do. And so on to our third stop which was similar to the first and about which we had few second thoughts. I felt we were getting nowhere fast so we pulled into a small cafe south of Auch for lunch and talked it through. I reminded Jonathan of our requirements and that these places had been far removed from what we were after. Jonathan is a charming fellow, quietly spoken, laid back and extremely clever.

He turned to me, apologised profusely for wasting our time, and said that he had one other place in mind but that it was the other side of Toulouse near a town called Lavaur. We looked at the map and saw that it was within our driving circle, quizzed him closely about it and said we would like to have a look. Later that evening he rang to say that he had arranged for us to see the place the day before we were due to fly home. I have never been able to decide whether his decision to drag us all the way out there to look at all those dreadful places was a clever ruse on his part – to soften us up – but on the 26th we were to find our future home.

Meanwhile we spent as much time as possible looking at the land south and south-west of Toulouse, even driving deep into the Pyrenees and looking back up the Garonne valley. It was indeed very beautiful and has attracted many British and other settlers but, for us, it was just a bit too far from Toulouse and too sparsely populated. It would be very difficult for Tristan and maybe a drive too far for many of our potential clients who would be with us for a short time only. On Christmas Eve we moved into Toulouse and booked in to a small hotel right in the heart of the city – Place du Capitole – where we spent the afternoon and evening idling around soaking up the atmosphere of the place.

As a rule I detest all cities and am filled with dread when Rachel orders me to accompany her on a shopping expedition, but there was something about this lovely, ancient city that caught the imagination. Even in late December it is possible to sit outside a cafe, comfortably warm and watch the world go by.

Most of the students had left for Christmas but there was still a youthful bustle about the festive crowds. Toulouse is a very cosmopolitan city and every nationality seemed to be represented. It was lively, gay (in the traditional sense of the word!) and had a vibrance about it. Buskers and street jugglers were playing to the crowds in the main squares, the shops were full and the city had an aura of well-being about it.

It was only later that we realised what enormous changes were taking place in and around Toulouse due to the development of the high technology and aerospace industries that we had heard about. Concorde had been built there several years ago but now the giant international consortium building Airbus aircraft had taken over.

Posing a direct challenge to Boeing as the world's leading aircraft manufacturer, Airbus had gathered around it a whole host of satellite industries, which had, in turn, created yet others and drawn in more from around the world. In a word Toulouse was not only surviving the changes to modern society that so often destroy great cities – it was becoming rich. Money was being poured into the city not only by France but by worldwide investment.

A short time before our arrival the airport had doubled in size, the motorway systems had been completed and huge new industrial estates had sprung up around the city. However, to their eternal credit, the city elders took great trouble to protect the beauty of the city centre, encircled to the west by the River Garonne and to the north and east by the Canal du Midi. Care was being taken of the city, the great changes to the place were being made sympathetically and in harmony with the Toulouse of old.

Massive underground car parks, capable of swallowing more than 10,000 vehicles spared the city from the worst ravages of the internal combustion engine, parks and open spaces were developed and the opera house and Halle aux Grains concert hall were refurbished. These two centres of music later drew us like magnets time and again when we found it almost impossible to get away for a holiday together. We chose instead to spend what pocket money we had on season tickets for the opera and for the occasional concert.

Lavaur lies just twenty-five miles or so from Toulouse and the house we were due to see was a few minutes the other side. The journey was short and uneventful and we drove slowly into the small market town. It is a typical country town such as one might find anywhere in rural England with a population of some 7,000, catering for the local farming community. It appeared to have everything we wanted and, in particular, a well-known and successful middle school and *lycée*.

We passed through the Centre Ville and went out on the Castres road before turning off towards the little hamlet of Massac. Here there was just a school, the mairie, a church and a collection of farms and cottages. Our destination was the far side of the hamlet and we turned left off the main road into a long shallow valley of farmland, the hilltops covered with woods.

At the head of the valley was a large wood and there, tucked beneath the trees, standing in its own grounds was a big house surrounded by a number of outbuildings. Smoke was curling up from the chimney. As we pulled up a friendly old dog came to meet us, barking huskily as old dogs do and escorted us to the front door. We had arrived at the 300-year-old *manoir* of the hamlet, a place that had been home to the last three *maires* of Massac-Seran – its name was Bosc Lebat.

The lady of the house had been widowed some two years previously and now, her children grown up and left home, she found the place far too big. She had put it on the market and after a short time it had attracted a number of potential buyers. Two of these had been British, one had wanted to open a shooting school but, mercifully, was denied permission. The thought of this lovely peaceful valley resounding to the crash of guns all day, day after day, defied the imagination.

The second party, having agreed to buy and arranged to meet at the *Notaire's* had simply failed to turn up, leaving the good lady bewildered, angry and somewhat suspicious of the British. However we were received with good grace and shown around the house, the outbuildings and gardens, after which we were invited to wander at leisure.

I said nothing to Rachel at the time but I felt my pulse quicken. Most houses leave you relatively unmoved, whilst others are sometimes cold, sending shivers down the spine, giving you the creeps. You are tempted to glance back over your shoulder furtively, half expecting to see a curtain draw back or a shadowy figure at a window. But, every now and then, you come across a house that seems to beckon and smile. Walk into the hallway and there is a feeling of warmth about the place and this was the case here.

I felt I was being drawn towards the house but then kicked myself for allowing sentiment to get the better of me. It was my impulsive Irish nature at work again. What about all those points we had talked through and what about the state of this place? This looked as though it might be the sort of property we were looking for and it would be better if I concentrated on the job in hand rather than daydreaming about what might be.

However, try as I might, I could not take my eyes off the place. Bosc Lebat was like one of those very rare, exceptionally beautiful women who, though perhaps a shade past their prime, still make men of all ages go weak at the knees. By this time Rachel was trying out her French on our hostess and two daughters. I managed to pick up that she was asking about Lavaur, schools, hairdressers and other matters of social and domestic importance. This, I thought, was a good omen.

Sometime later she told me that while they were talking the telephone had rung. After taking the call the owner came back into the room and announced casually that she had just received another enquiry about the house. Strangely enough this did not cause us any bother but, if it had not been cleverly stage-managed, it was an almost unbelievable coincidence – with perfect timing.

Later, once we had settled in, we got to know our predecessor and one of her daughters who now lives and works in Toulouse. They told us that they had moved down from Brittany some twenty-five years previously. Monsieur was an agricultural advisor and, as he did not need all the land at Bosc Lebat, sold much of it and put the money into modernising the house and buildings. He became immensely popular with the local farmers whom he helped, showing them modern agricultural methods and introducing them to new machinery, fertilizers and chemicals.

The six children – three boys and three girls – had a wonderful early life, running free in the woods and fields, often walking barefoot to the village through the tall grass and carpets of wild flowers by the side of the track. The big homestead remained almost self-supporting and had its own poultry, goats, house cows and working animals. I could well imagine the idyllic family life here: a marvellous place in which to be brought up as a young child.

The drive back to Toulouse was completed in almost total silence and I cannot remember the house being mentioned until we were back in the hotel. 'Well, come on,' I said, 'what did you make of it all?'

'It was nice,' she replied in that maddening way women do, leaving so much unsaid.

'Well, go on. What did you like best about it?' I pressed.

'The warmth of the place. There was a lovely feel about the house. It seemed to be asking us to come and live there. Yes, there was something about it,' she murmured.

'That's the Irish in you,' I quipped.

'Well what did you make of it?'

'All that and more,' I confessed. We looked at each other across the room and knew that our thoughts were as one – our minds were made up.

Looking back it was sheer madness. I was still in the Army, we both had houses in England but not one penny more. We had only just glimpsed the place and yet here we were seeing ourselves as the owners already. We were due to fly back the following afternoon but felt that we must get back out there for a second look in the morning. I had no idea where we ate that evening or what was on the menu, for our minds were fixed on Bosc Lebat and on what we were going to see the next day. We talked late into the night and told ourselves that in the morning we had to be sensible and practical. We must not on any account get carried away by it all.

In the event it was all very much as the day before and we wandered around looking here and there, trying to hoist in what was wrong with the place rather than being seduced by the magic of it. Rachel stayed indoors to ask more questions about domestic matters and I escaped into the gardens and orchards, poking around the numerous barns and outbuildings. I moved around slowly, trying to take in all I could see until I had circled the homestead and returned once more to the front lawn. It was about midday and the sun, even then in mid-winter, was warm on my back as I paused and leant against the back of a bench on the lawn.

I looked up at the old house, gazing at the solid, dignified features of the building and my mind wandered back to the long and turbulent history of this area. I found myself wondering just how much of the past this ancient dwelling – now nearly 300 years old – had witnessed. It would have been a hundred years old or more, at least, at the time of the

Revolution. What, I wondered, would have been the effect of those terrible times on the household?

Without doubt they would have been a family of some local importance who might have held widely differing views about the removal of the monarchy and nobility from those around them. Indeed they may have known many who were sought out and slaughtered during the years of the *Terreurs*: perhaps some of those living here might have been taken and executed. The family and servants living here could not have remained unaffected by all that was taking place around them.

Some years later Wellington's army would have passed this way and fought the Battle of Toulouse just a few miles away. Would those living here have heard the rumble of the artillery in the distance? What stories would they have heard about the battle? Might British scouting patrols have come to the house after the battle or might some of the wounded been brought to large houses such as this? Would there have been hatred and fear in the minds of the inhabitants or would they, once the fighting had stopped, have taken pity on those who lay here, whatever their nationality?

And what about more recent events when another army dominated this peaceful and inoffensive corner of France, this time an army of brutal occupation? Without doubt patrols from the Das Reich Division would have driven up the valley in their search for Resistance fighters, perhaps bringing with them sinister members of the Gestapo from their local headquarters in Toulouse.

The Maquis were busy around here, sometimes striking at the invaders, sometimes helping allied servicemen avoid capture on their way to Spain. Brave men operated from out of the hills and woods in those dark days. It was easy to imagine some members of the household slipping away in the night on some mission or other, the failure of which or capture would have meant certain death often after cruel torture.

The old house would have seen all of this and much more besides – births, marriages, deaths, good times and hard times, the house would have seen tears and laughter over the years. Before the present house was built there would have been earlier dwellings here, stretching far back into history: before the extermination of the Cathars in the thirteenth century, before even Caesar's legionaires tramped along the high ridge behind me.

Looking up at the house I felt like a small child looking into the strong, kind face of an old man whose twinkling eyes and creased features had seen the rich, full pattern of life – good times and bad. Just like that small child I felt warm, comfortable and secure with the face that was looking down at me. The front door opened and I started from my dreams as Rachel appeared with the owners who had come to bid us farewell.

On our way back we compared notes and neither of us had found anything untoward. That afternoon, on the plane, I tried to look objectively at it all by comparing what we had just seen with the imperatives we had given ourselves.

1. It had to be within 45 minutes of a major communication centre – in this case Toulouse. Having given ourselves this limitation it was interesting to note that if we had found something much closer to the airport we would have become entangled with all the developing urbanisation and industrial estates. It seemed perfect.

2. It had to less than 10 minutes from the centre of a decent-sized town – Lavaur. Bosc Lebat was an ideal distance from the market town. We were within easy striking distance yet not caught up in all the life and traffic at the edge of the town.

3. The house had to be in a good position. Bosc Lebat was at the eastern end of our valley where it lay protected from the north and east weather by the hills behind. The house was south facing and there was a lovely view across open farmland up to the far ridge in the distance.

4. The house had to be in good condition. This was something of a worry as we had both seen a number of things that had to be put right. However there were numerous positive aspects and as long as we sold

our own homes well and as long as the pound remained high we should be able to manage.

5. The house had to have dignity and style. We were not after a *Grand Manoir* or Chateau but we did want a place where our guests would have space and not be on top of one another. Bosc Lebat had all that.

6. It had to be big enough for our requirements. Again, we were happy with this.

7. Finally, and most important of all, it had to be within our budget. Already we had catered for the purchase price, agents' and *notaire's* fees, our move and a substantial reserve. There seemed to be no problem here.

We felt that we had come a long way in a short time and the decision now was whether to go ahead with Bosc Lebat or wait, get out there and rent a place while having a good look around in slow time. This would have been the preferred way to go about it, however, if we wanted to do this we had to decide now which town we wanted to be near. We had decided to bring Tristan out with us and he would have to start school right away. The last thing we wanted to do was to settle him in one school only to move on somewhere else a few months later.

We were happy that Lavaur suited our requirements admirably so the question was whether or not we would be able to find anything better than Bosc Lebat within the small area we had drawn around the town. We both felt that this was unlikely so our mind was made up – press ahead now with Bosc Lebat and get the show on the road.

The year 1992 was an immensely busy time. We sold Rachel's cottage, put her furniture into store and she moved into Winchester. She was still teaching so the grand piano came along as well and our dining room became a temporary *salon de musique*. Soon after this we heard that the first redundancy announcements had been made.

Her Majesty was happy to release me from my contract and I decided that my last day of duty would be the day before my 50th birthday at the end of September. We remained in close touch with Jonathan and began to talk prices with him. We felt that the asking price was rather too high and, after the usual session of long-range haggling, we managed to entice Madame down a bit and clinched the deal, promising to come out again in the summer to sign the *Compromis de Vente* before completing in November.

Times had indeed been hectic but throughout it all Rachel and I reckoned that it was high time to get on with our own affairs and made plans to get married on 26 June in Winchester. We dashed up to Norfolk to see her family and then down to Devon where my parents also laid on a party for us.

We thought we should take a break from it all and went down to Wales for a walking weekend in the high, wild Brecons. The great hills were as impressive as ever and we dutifully battled our way to the top of Pen y Fan, the highest peak. It was a trip down memory lane and brought back many memories of the special forces selection courses in which the great hills had featured so prominently. It was a marvellous break, but only too brief for we had get back to the planning as time was moving on.

Our wedding was a quiet affair attended by a few members of the family and some friends, however, there was no time for a honeymoon as we had to get back out to France to sign the necessary papers. For some time we had been concerned about the legal aspects of such a venture. Several books have been written about buying properties in France and there were a number of horror stories circulating about the problems that might be encountered. The trick in all this was to get a reliable agent and a reputable *notaire* who would lead both parties through the legal jungle step by step.

We felt quite secure with Jonathan but knew nothing about the *notaire* who had been selected personally by the vendor. When we heard this little red warning lights began to flash and we felt that we should have a friend in court. In the event we need not have worried, for the *notaire* was a charming man who lead us carefully and patiently through the whole business. In fact he knew Bosc Lebat well having spent some time there as a boy with the children of the house. Later when we used him to buy some adjoining land he amused us with stories of his boyhood when he used to play around the house and grounds.

The experience served as a warning that we should find ourselves a good solicitor on whom we could call should there be problems in the future. There are a number of highly qualified British solicitors working in France and we have found a splendid one working in Toulouse. One of the very few to be qualified in English and French law, Belinda is bilingual and now works for the Toulouse branch of a Paris law firm. She and William have become good friends and we often laugh at the memories of us stumbling around nervously in those early days.

Later, once we had settled, Rachel would occasionally take a short break from the routine at Bosc Lebat. She would arrange to meet Belinda for lunch at one of the little restaurants or pavement cafes when the two of them would sit and chat for a couple of hours whilst the world passed by. Both claimed it allowed them to escape for a while and, later still, French friends would join them when they would all chatter away, swap stories and laugh about the little things that had come into their lives.

After lunch Rachel would wander slowly through the city perhaps gazing at some of the lovely things in the shops, perhaps visiting an art gallery or museum with a friend, sometimes even she would just wander wherever her feet took her, absorbing the sights, the sounds and the atmosphere of the great city. She would feel the Frenchness of the little squares, the shops and the open parks.

The whole melange of Toulousain life, from the wealth and affluence on the main boulevards to the cosmopolitan and bohemian nature of the students and artists would exhilarate her. Invariably she would return refreshed from her day out and cheered by those she had met, where they had lunched and what they had all done.

Eventually our trips into Toulouse for the opera or concerts became great treats. Every four or five weeks we would leave home and drive to the city for lunch in one of the restaurants around Place Wilson or Place St George. Sometimes we would be alone, on other occasions we would meet up with friends. Once the leisurely lunch was over we would wander slowly through the centre to the Opera House for the matinee. After the performance we would pause a while for a coffee or aperitif in Place du Capitole before driving home to supper.

Rachel would make me study the work we were going to see before we left home and we would discuss the plot or some major part of the work in the car on the way in. Gradually the world of music came to mean something to me. I had heard many of the arias or choruses before but in isolation only, and to see and hear them now on the stage as the story unfolded was a whole new experience. Rather than a chore to be avoided, a journey into this particular city would become something I would look forward to.

All this was, of course, some way off, and on this first visit we could little more than get a feel for Toulouse and compare it with other large cities we knew. Later that evening, after night had fallen, we went out again and sauntered down to the river, walking along the embankment gazing out over the water at Pont Neuf and Pont St Michel dressed with fairy lights. Even then it seemed as though Toulouse would not only provide us with all our requirements but would be a delightful place to explore in time to come.

We had chosen to come out for the signing during the holiday of 14 July – Bastille Day – when the whole of France remembers the most critical moment of The Revolution. The country closes down for a short break and the whole population sets about the business of enjoying itself. We had booked in to a small hotel in Lavaur and, after dinner, decided to walk up to the beautiful little fourteenth-century cathedral to watch the fireworks and other celebrations. On our way there we joined the crowds who had gathered first to watch the inevitable bicycle races around the town and to cheer on the local lads.

Someone was doing his best to tell us who was doing what through an ancient loudspeaker system but the excitement of the occasion got to him and he was yelling into the machine at the top of his voice. The old instrument retaliated by emitting a series of piercing whistles, the whole commentary being rendered quite unintelligible. The crowds loved it, however, and the young heroes were cheered all the way to the line. Across the wide, tree-lined avenue on the main boulevard a fair was in full swing, the plaintive strains of an accordion mingling with the aroma of a thousand Gaullois on the warm evening air combined to remind us that we were indeed deep in southern France.

We walked slowly towards the cathedral of St Alain which stands next to the Mairie. Both look out onto well-tended public gardens and are set on a bluff high above the River Agout that passes through Lavaur on its way to join the larger River Tarn at St Sulpice. It was a wonderful, family affair and everywhere large groups had gathered with friends for the occasion. Sometimes three or even four generations of one family would sit talking together or stroll quietly up and down the main boulevard, the smallest children up aloft on fathers' shoulders.

Perhaps Lavaur was just a sleepy little hollow but it suited us perfectly and we soon warmed to the place. The fireworks were despatched from all corners of the cathedral, swishing their way into the night sky before exploding in a crescendo of flashes and bangs. The crowds gasped, clapped and shouted their approval before everyone made their way back into town where the bandstand, overlooking a huge wooden dance floor, had become the centre of attraction. The band played the songs and dances of byegone years as the local folk spun, twirled and stepped out to the old favourites. Lavaur, it seemed to us, was a happy place, the people cheerful and happy too.

At the end of our long evening, we paused on a seat under some trees on the boulevard that leads off the main square in the Centre Ville. Across the road a group of youngsters were sitting quietly around some tables outside a cafe enjoying the cool of the late evening. All of a sudden we heard them singing 'Joyeux Anniversaire!' and, as the last strains of the song faded away, several leapt to their feet and surrounded a young girl as she sat in her chair. With a loud cheer she was picked up,

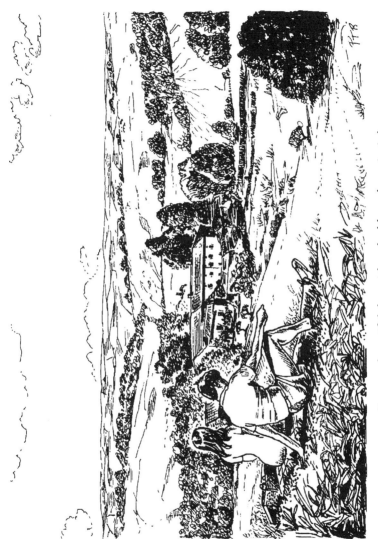

'It was a beautiful day and we had brought a picnic.'

held aloft and taken across to the pond surrounding the fountain. There, still in her chair, the Birthday Girl was lowered gently into the water squealing her loud protestations even as she disappeared under the fountain waters to the delight of the late-night revellers.

The next morning, following the signing, we went out to Bosc Lebat again. Not to the house this time but up into the surrounding hills from where we could look down and gaze on what was now virtually ours. It was a beautiful day and we had brought a picnic lunch out with us. There were still so many questions to answer and so many imponderables that we just wanted to sit there quietly and take it all in. It was an exciting moment, we were both thrilled at what we saw below us and with the decision we had made, yet perhaps a touch apprehensive at what lay ahead.

I remembered a similar sensation when standing in the door of a Hercules aircraft, hooked up and ready to jump. I had done everything possible to make sure it would all work out. If it did then things would be marvellous, if not – it could get mighty painful! We spent a quiet hour or two up there wondering about how this or that might go and about our plans for the house such as they were, before coming away cautiously optimistic about the future and what lay ahead.

# CHAPTER V

# Preparing and Moving South

*The Shaws and all their advice. As the Pound crashes.*
*Preparations at home. Leaving the Army. Some hard farewells.*

Some time before our visit we had been put in touch with a couple who had bought a chateau in the Gers, west of Toulouse, and who were doing what we intended to do. We had given them a call and they had asked us over to stay for a couple of nights. Sir Archie and Sarah Shaw had bought a beautiful chateau about an hour to the west of Auch. Set amidst some 150 acres of its own farmland it faced due south over the countryside of the Gers towards the mountains in the distance.

Just as we were intending to do, they had decided to sell up in England and had moved, lock, stock and barrel, to a new life in southern France. They had made the move some three years previously, had restored their new home and their business was now up and running. They were, so we were reliably informed, just the people to whom we should talk. It was altogether a much larger enterprise than ours but they went out of their way to tell us about the mysteries of the business. It was something quite new to us but they were old hands by now.

Archie met us dressed, as always, in a sloppy old sweater, slippers, glass in hand and the inevitable pipe going full blast. Years before he had been a pilot of some distinction in the Royal Navy and throughout the chateau one would stumble across mementoes of his flying days. Now in his sixties, Archie was in his element, drifting around his lovely old home, keeping the guests amused with his yarns, he was obviously loving every minute of it.

Sarah was, and still is, a veritable dynamo, bustling here and there keeping everything up to the mark. Not content with just B&B, they had started to farm the land and she was considering opening up her own property business. We thought we had taken on a lot but this was altogether a different league.

After lunch Sarah sat us down and started to talk about the business – the fun and the laughter we would have, together with the problems and possible horrors that we might encounter. We sat there for what seemed like hours, listening intently to her stories. From time to time Archie would appear jabbing the air with his pipe as he underlined some point that Sarah had made. It was fascinating stuff and we tried to remember it all for it was surely going to stand us in good stead in the times ahead.

The first point she made concerned the danger of being swamped by visitors. 'Everybody but everybody down here has suffered from this,' she claimed. 'None of us know why it is but as soon as you get a place in France everybody at home seems to think that you are stinking rich and have got an ever open door. My advice to you is to get your act together before you start. Work out in your mind exactly who comes for free, who can have very special rates, who gets just a little bit off and the rest have to pay in full or you will just go under. You cannot pay for their holidays.'

This was stern stuff and the more we thought about it the more we realised how difficult this was going to be. Later when we were at Bosc Lebat we heard the same story again and again. One British family had been overrun by no less than ninety people in their very first year. Family, friends, even mere nodding acquaintances, happened to be 'passing through' as they put it and nearly all of them had decided to break their holiday for two or three days.

Archie came in and endorsed what Sarah had been saying. 'The buggers descend on you giving the impression that they've been good enough to break their holiday just for your benefit. They eat you out of house and home and then push off leaving you to clear up the mess, pay the bills and get yourselves ready for the next lot. Honestly, watch this one like a hawk. One or two are fine and its always good to see them but once the word gets out that you are open and up for grabs, they come in their droves!'

Rachel and I took this point on board determined not to allow this to happen. But it was going to be tricky getting the right balance. In England we all went off and stayed with friends and they came and stayed with us. Cost never came into it – perhaps a bottle of whisky and a bunch of flowers but that would be it. Somehow, without upsetting our friends or sounding too mercenary, we had to get the message across that this was now our livelihood. Put another way, if we were running an antique business or an art gallery no one would expect us to give away freebees or even discounts, but from now on every bed filled for the night was going to be our bread and butter.

We were desperately hoping that our friends would indeed call and stay but we could not possibly afford to entertain everyone and what was left of the meagre pensions was not going to get us very far. Added to which if they came in the middle of the season we would not be able to spend much time with them and they would be tangled up with the other guests. This looked like being a difficult one.

Sarah's next point brought home the problems of renovating the new home. 'It will cost you twice as much as you were ever told and will take half as long again as the builders promised it would.' She went on to say that it was not the fault of the French artisans or the system, rather it was all to do with picking around old houses. Bosc Lebat was nearly 300 years old and built on clay. If we were going to knock holes in the walls and take up floors we were likely to discover some horrors, so we had better be prepared.

It was sound advice because even the most careful estimate could be made only on what was visible. No builder in his right mind was going to price himself out of a contract because he was generous enough to add in a fudge factor for what he might have to do. The other point was that once the builder was on site with his power tools, concrete mixer etc. he was often asked to do a number of other jobs that had not been included in the original estimate. So we were going to have to be careful, add in our own fudge factors and limit the artisan to what he had been engaged to do.

Archie and Sarah advised us to be very careful about black labour, especially British black labour. There were a number of issues here but, as Sarah pointed out, the main worry was that there was no guarantee and once the job had been done and the team paid in cash it would be the devil's own problem getting them back to put right anything that they had done badly.

Furthermore, if we were planning to have anything done to the electrics then a properly qualified electrician needed to be called in or the work would not be insured and if there was to be a fire, then what? The French authorities did not take kindly to piratical gangs of foreign black labour bucking the system, not paying their taxes and keeping good honest French boys out of work.

By the time the subject had got around to dealing with guests Archie had placed large, full glasses in front of us and we spent a hilarious time listening to their tales. It was clear that they enjoyed what they were doing and that the vast majority of guests were fun to have around, were interesting and wanted to make life as easy for their hosts as they possibly could. Archie made the point that the guests would not want to get out and about the whole time and that we should think about keeping those who wanted a quiet day in and around the house happy.

'Give them a playground,' he said waving towards the pool and tennis court. 'On occasions they just like to hang around, let their hair down and forget all about being some pompous Chief Executive of this or Chairman of that. Let them! You are not in the business of chasing them off the patch at 0900 like some Blackpool landlady. All they want to do is relax and who can blame them after flogging themselves to death all year? Just like a bunch of kids really. Give them somewhere to play boules, even table tennis and they will be as happy as sandboys.'

He pulled on his pipe, deep in thought before continuing, 'And don't bother to charge them for drinks – include it all in the house price. It's a pain in the arse trying to remember who has had what and, to be honest, its a bit infra dig going around after breakfast and asking everyone how many gin and tonics or glasses of vino they had last night. Even worse trying to get them to write down what they had, for God's sake! By the end of the evening they're all far too pissed and knackered to remember anything.'

It was all good stuff; obvious when thought about but good advice nonetheless on how to make things as civilised as possible for the guests. But occasionally an oddball would be bound to turn up or somebody would arrive at the front door who had suffered an unbearable journey and who needed to be jollied along until he was himself again. 'Well, you have to use your loaf here,' Archie retorted. 'You can usually tell who are the proper chaps that are just a bit hacked off with the day. But you don't want any professional moaners about the place.'

'And what happens if a visit turns into a complete can of worms?' I asked.

'Tell them to bugger off,' Archie replied. 'Seriously, this is your home not a ruddy hotel. If they can't play the game and behave themselves, you don't want them around the place.'

I looked at the old sea salt and could well imagine the scene when some nit-picking guest had gone too far, overstepped the mark and had received a broadside, most likely being told to stand up straight, get his feet together and get a haircut at the same time. However we had taken the point that there had to be a bottom line somewhere and if matters came to a head one could only ask them to leave. I offered up a silent prayer that we would not be put to this ultimate test at Bosc Lebat.

'Whilst talking about the guests, you want to think about advertising,' Sarah continued. 'You will have to work out what sort of guests you want to have around the place and ensure that you advertise where that sort of person will read your adverts. It's a costly business and a bit hit and miss so think about it.'

'Like fishing,' interrupted Archie. 'You wouldn't go after the leaping salmon in some gungy old clay pit on the outskirts of Brum. Nothing wrong with the folk up there, mind you. I once had a splendid manservant called Fred. He was a Brummie and a great bloke but he wouldn't be comfortable spending his holidays here with us in the chateau. Get the drift?'

We seemed to go on for hours chatting about this and that before eventually crawling into bed at some ungodly hour, our heads spinning with tales of horrendous problems, social minefields and a hundred and one contingency plans that would get us back onto the straight and narrow. But it had been an extremely successful session. In the end we managed to heed most of their advice but not all, much to our cost. Archie and Sarah have become good friends but, sadly, their beautiful home and Bosc Lebat are too far apart for anything other than the occasional visit.

Life was gathering pace in Winchester and the thought that we had signed for a house in south-west France concentrated our minds. All we had to do now was to pay for the place and get ourselves out there. We had decided not to complete on Bosc Lebat until I was out of the Army and had my redundancy settlement in the bank and we had sold my own place in Winchester.

This called for careful timing as I needed to find a buyer for my house and this was none too easy as house prices had peaked in the summer and were now falling away sharply. I decided to sell the place myself and placed an advertisement in the local papers and national press after I had written out a set of particulars and added one or two photographs. We were lucky and found a buyer almost immediately who was prepared to adjust his timings to suit our needs. We now had our finances sorted and all that was required was a trip to the bank to buy the necessary number of Francs.

\*   \*   \*

Towards the end of summer in 1992 the Pound was coming under increasing speculative pressure. Throughout the time we had been preparing ourselves for the move it had been riding high at around Ff9.6 per Pound, until the infamous Black Monday in October 92 when it was taken out of the ERM and allowed to find its own level. It promptly crashed to around Ff8.0 exactly at the time we had arranged to convert our precious Pounds into Francs and we watched in horror as the Pound fell by almost 20 per cent in the space of a couple of days.

We had, of course, put down a deposit on Bosc Lebat and were thus more or less committed. It was a very painful moment that tested our resolve and just before walking down to Lloyds Bank we had a final glance at the price of Sterling on the telly – it was down to Ff8.01.

'Come on,' I said putting my arm around Rachel. 'Let's get on with it but if it has fallen any lower when we get to the bank we will pull out of it.'

We walked nervously into the bank and were ushered into a small side office by the official who was to make the transaction for us. He explained how he proposed to set about it, telling us that he would call up London and find out the exact exchange rate. He would then confirm with us the amount that we wanted to buy and that we still wanted to proceed. If we agreed he would instruct London to buy and that would be that. No going back.

It all had a chillingly familiar ring to it and took my mind back to when I was working in NATO for the Commander-in-Chief. We were deep underground in the war bunker somewhere in southern Germany rehearsing the global release of nuclear weapons. When the moment came the great man was confronted by a small team of US experts who were about to invite him to press some sinister-looking buttons. Before doing so they issued a terrible warning that, once the dreaded deed was done, that would be that. There would be no going back or second chance. 'Once you give me the nod, General, that's it. Moscow's flattened!' That was only an exercise – thank God – but right now, here in Lloyds Bank, Winchester it was for real.

Our man duly called up London and confirmed that the exchange rate was Ff8.01. Rachel and I looked at each other, smiled weakly and nodded, at which moment we became the proud owners of two million French francs but every single last penny of my redundancy package had disappeared down the plug along with the bath water. It was a very tough moment but we had done it and now, to all intents and purposes, we had crossed our Rubicon.

The next few months passed in a blur of activity well known to anyone who has undertaken a complicated move from one country to another. I should add that right up to the point we bought the money I was still in the Army. I had left Netheravon some time previously and was posted to the main School of Infantry to see out the last few months of my career. Leaving Netheravon was sad. It was my last command and it had been a happy and satisfying time.

As I cleared my office I took my military plaques off the wall to pack them for the move. The last one down was the School of Infantry emblem of a bayonet embossed on a red shield. Now, so it seemed, some thirty-three years after joining the Army as an infantryman, my bayonet was going back into its scabbard for the last time.

The officers were kind enough to lay on a superb dinner and a number of old friends were present. After the meal, as on all the best Dinner Nights, they let their hair down and played all manner of games in and around the Officers' Mess. There was one game though which they did not know and which I remembered from my very first days in Plymouth.

There was no name for it but it involved two players, a shotgun and one cartridge. Somebody went off and warned the camp guard that there would be gunfire coming from the Officers' Mess but they were not to worry. High spirits you understand! The IRA were still prowling around the place and we did not wish fire to be returned in our direction by an over-enthusiastic guard.

The shotgun would be broken down and laid on the ground outside the front door with the cartridge beside it. Two officers would be summoned – one sometimes might be a visiting senior officer, the other a junior officer from the home team. The President for the evening would arrange the two officers side by side close to the gun.

A coin would be tossed to see which officer was to be shot at. Then, on the command 'Go', the loser would begin running for his life whilst the winner had the pleasure of assembling the gun, loading it and letting fly at the figure disappearing down the drive. It was amazing to see how fast an officer could run after a heavy meal, plenty to drink, and clad in the tight, restrictive evening dress. It was great fun and nobody got hurt, but it was wise to have a sober referee present in case the officer who was supposed to run away tripped over his spurs and fell over in panic, whilst the one with the gun got carried away with enthusiasm.

As the moment of departure approached so the amount of paperwork grew and we embarked upon the seemingly endless task of disconnecting ourselves from everything British and going into a state of limbo, living for a while rather like gypsies, before reappearing in France and locking ourselves into the French system. The one most adversely affected was poor old Patch who, in order to comply with the mad, bureaucratic nightmare imposed on us by the Ministry of Agriculture, was treated as though he was some pampered supreme champion. Yet, on the day, the extremely bored official simply waved Patch and all his hard-won documents through without bothering to get off his seat.

We were now almost ready and the time had come to bid farewell to family and friends. We both found that saying goodbye to the family was more difficult than we had ever imagined. Leaving elderly parents is never easy and on this occasion we all knew that visits were going to be infrequent although we were within relatively easy striking distance.

Even if you do not see too much of the family while at home you can at least get into the car and drive to a family gathering or crisis. From now on this was not going to be the case and our parents, whilst still all in good health, were getting on in years. Parting from the family was a cross we had to bear if we were going to be living way down in southern France.

A few years previously I had been through much the same thing with my brother. Hugh had decided to row the Atlantic single handed and was making his final preparations in Tenerife when I flew out to see him. We spent a few precious days together before I had to leave him to it. Parting like that was very tough and as we bade farewell at the airport both of us knew what dangers he was about to face. We clasped each other firmly praying that this would not be our last moment together. In the event he made it, arriving in Barbados exactly one hundred days after setting out – just one tin of bully beef and a small can of rancid water left in the boat. However, I knew only too well how difficult these family moments would be for us all.

Parting from the young was, for both of us, even harder. Hugo was at university in Portsmouth and Jamie had just begun his training at a college near London. Thelma, their mother, was still in Ulster albeit on the point of returning, so they were going to be on their own for some time. Looking back now I realise that, whilst still at college or university, the young remain in a relatively safe and controlled environment. It is the years immediately after which are so difficult, when they step into the wide world with no safe haven, free from the last vestiges of guidance. They are then truly on their own and have to fend for themselves.

All well and good if they are going on to an organised environment such as the armed services or some other major organisation, or if they are fortunate enough to move straight into a secure and well-paid job. But for many it is not so easy and both Hugo and Jamie found their first few years after college difficult. Dan, Rachel's elder son, was still with his father in Basingstoke whilst Tristan was coming with us.

He had a long struggle ahead of him for he was to go straight into the French middle school in Lavaur and throughout the last few months we gave him as much extra French language training as he could take. In the end his schooling was a great success but right then he too must have been wondering quietly how things were going to work out and if he would be able to cope.

We moved out at the end of October, stayed with some friends nearby and headed for the ferry at Portsmouth on a dull, chilly autumn evening where we met up with Hugo for a last farewell. We all had our private thoughts as we stood at the rail whilst the ferry slipped her moorings. We were not going to the Yukon or Papua New Guinea and if the worst came to the worst we could retrace our steps without too much difficulty. But we were on our way to a new life nonetheless and it would be a strange person indeed who did not have a few moments of self-doubt at what might be in store.

# CHAPTER VI

# *Home Sweet Home*

*We arrive, complete and take possession. Drains and Odd Job.*
*British builders and French artisans. The pool goes in. Advertising.*

All sea ports at dawn in late October are fairly bleak places and Caen was no exception. Perhaps it was the chill blustery wind or even some new concession to free movement throughout the EEC, but there was neither sight nor sound of any customs officials save the one portly fellow tucked snugly into his little box – and after all we had done to get things right. We did not waste any time looking for them, but kept our heads down, got the whip out and sped for the exit as fast as we could.

Rather than go all the way down to Lavaur in one go we broke the journey for a couple of nights with some old friends who had set out on their adventure some months before us and who were now well ensconced in their new home at Languidic near Lorient on the Breton coast. The car was loaded to the roof, with Tristan and Patch shoe-horned into the back, and we were pulling a small trailer containing our essential bits and pieces. It was impossible to cover the ground very fast so we broke the journey once again before eventually pulling in to Lavaur on the afternoon of 5 November.

The small hotel we had used in the summer has served us well. The Jacquemart is friendly and well placed, tucked away in a long row of buildings alongside the old corn exchange, beside a little terrace. As we pulled in Jean-Claude and Michèle Decoux, the owners, came out and greeted us warmly. 'Welcome back,' they cried, 'and this time it's for good!'

We were due to complete the purchase in the morning but the previous owner had been kind enough to leave a barn open in which we could store anything we wanted for the night. Tristan and I drove out to the house just as it was getting dark to park up the trailer. After unhitching we walked slowly around the buildings, now locked and shuttered. It was a dark evening and very still and I pointed out what I could remember of the layout to him.

The Guardian's House is at the the far side of the courtyard and as we walked around to the back we heard noises in the undergrowth. There was a rustling as though some large animal was pushing its way around in the bushes and then we heard the grunts and squeals of pigs or, in this case, wild boar. We stood still trying to determine which way the beasts were going but saw nothing and gradually the noises faded into the distance as the creatures went on their way.

Later we were to learn that Bosc Lebat is on one of the boars' migratory routes. They travel between the high limestone crags of the Black Mountains to our east where they go in the spring to have their young, and then move back to the great forests beyond Gaillac where they winter on acorns and chestnuts. They had been using this route since the dawn of history and we had come upon this family as they moved across to their winter feeding grounds to our north.

Boar are shy creatures that lie up during the day using the cover of darkness to feed and move across country. Stories abound of their savagery and the vicious, unprovoked attacks they can make. Usually, however, they do all they can to avoid contact with man and only attack when they feel threatened or have been wounded – and who can blame them for that?

Back in the hotel we settled down for the evening with our hosts who went out of their way to tell us about our new home town. Not only did they run the Jacquemart but Jean-Claude had built a large reception hall down by the river and between the two institutions the Decoux had an insight to all that went on in and around Lavaur. After supper we moved into the front bar and listened to their views on what was what in the town.

Across the road was the market place and not much news or gossip missed the Jaquemart on market days when farmers and stallholders alike came in for a cafe or aperitif. Jean-Claude heard most of what went on from his position behind the bar and what did not come his way was gleaned by Michèle as she organised lunch in the restaurant.

They became good friends and, in those early, difficult days, gave us some excellent advice and helped us find our way around the shops and businesses in town. We see them often now, Jean-Claude, either standing four square behind his bar or striding purposefully through the town, grey locks flying in the breeze and Michèle, her trim figure bustling here and there, remain an important part of the Lavaur scene for us.

The next day, 6 November 1992, Bosc Lebat was ours. The completion of the paperwork took place under the watchful eye of the *notaire*, there were handshakes all round and we were handed the keys to our new home. We hurried back as fast as we could with the last owner who, having opened the doors, then rushed around the house throwing open the shutters with a great flourish.

The removal team was due to arrive the following day so we busied ourselves working out what and who was going where, exploring as much as we could and unpacking the trailer before going back for a last night in Lavaur. It all looked so very different to what we had seen on our earlier visit and we could see that we were going to be busy for some time to come.

Our plan was to get unpacked and settled then give ourselves three months in which administration, bureaucracy and paperwork would have priority. During this period we would take stock of what had to be done to our domain and, rather than attacking things willy nilly, would work out a list of essential tasks for both the house and outbuildings while we sorted out our administration. After that we would turn our full attention to the house and go flat out to get some sort of order into things, aiming to get at least one room in the house ready for guests.

We realised too that we needed the pool to be in and the *gîte* ready by the summer. The cause of this horrific timetable was the crash of the Pound which had all but wiped out our financial reserve. Because of this we had no choice but to get ourselves ready for the coming summer season in the hope that at least some guests would stay and bring in a bit of income. Anything was going to be a bonus but we set out determined to get the business running within eight months.

The removal team arrived on schedule in one enormous lorry towing an equally large trailer. We heard the lorry groaning its way up the road before turning into the drive but after that – silence. I went outside and found the lorry and trailer had got halfway up the drive, had stopped but were leaning over dangerously towards the trees. They were so heavy that they had sunk into the gravel drive and looked most unlikely to move until they had been emptied. Everything had to be manhandled up the drive, then up a long flight of steps and into the house. There were just two men and how they worked.

The five of us walked through the house together, deciding where and how we were going to start. The very first task, we all agreed, was to dig out the beds, set them up and get them ready for the night. We knew full well that, at the end of this particular day, we would just want to collapse where we were and not start hunting around in the dark for the box containing the bed linen.

Rachel arranged her kitchen then disappeared into Lavaur to get some lunch and supper. Tristan started work on his room and I busied myself unpacking the first of the boxes the two men brought into the house. It was a long day, just as tiring as we had all predicted and, come nightfall, we were only too glad to down tools and assemble in the kitchen for our first meal under the new roof.

Rachel and I had already decided that, eventually, we were going to live downstairs in the suite behind the kitchen, but for the first few weeks we slept in the small double room at the back of the house. It was a cosy little room with a view out over the courtyard, past the *pigeonnier* to the hills behind. The bed faced the large window and, when finally we got there late that night we just lay still looking out into the night for no curtains were yet fixed and the shutters were open.

The old house had seen moves such as this many times before. Work had now stopped, there were no voices and no movement, yet in the quiet of the night, we could hear creaks and groans as the house settled. Sometimes a water pipe would burble, sometimes a stair or a floorboard creaked and occasionally there would be a rustle behind the walls or in the attic above our heads as a mouse or some other small night creature went about its business.

We lay silently, each with our own thoughts, gazing out at the mass of stars in the clear northern sky, the walls of the courtyard bathed grey in the bright moonlight. I reached out, found her hand and gently closed my fingers around hers. Her fingers tightened in response, she moved closer to me and said quietly, 'Well, here we are. What do you think? Do you think everything is going to be alright?'

'It's got to be,' I replied. 'There's no going back now – is there?' Silence again as the enormity of it all sank in. 'What are you thinking about?' I asked softly.

'Oh, all the obvious things – home, the family, the boys. It all seems so far away now, and here there's so much to do. What about you?' she asked.

'Just the same,' I replied. 'We'll make it all right but it's a little bit sad just now.' We both shared the same mixture of feelings – a touch nostalgic about all that we had left behind, yet excitement at the thought of what lay ahead. Moments later thoughts of home or the next day vanished abruptly as the harsh cry of a barn owl on the ledge outside broke the silence, making us start.

Bosc Lebat, as we were soon to find, had many occupants and the owls were amongst the most vociferous. Lying there it seemed almost as if this beautiful bird had flown across the courtyard from the old *pigeonnier* especially to call on us and to reassure us that we were not on our own.

'To call and reassure us that we were not on our own.'

75

A minute later, out in the field beyond the wood we heard the cry of a vixen but that was all. Exhausted and too tired even to whisper to one another, we simply curled up and fell deeply asleep not stirring till long after dawn.

The removal men stayed with us for two days, working steadily away hour after hour, declining our offer of beds in the house, choosing instead to sleep in the lorry. They took their meals with us and we did what we could to show our appreciation for all they did. We had taken some trouble in selecting a reliable and well-known removal firm; not only had all our effects been packed carefully and handled with care but the men were determined to see everything safely in and unpacked. There was no rush against the clock, no short cuts were taken and we were indebted to them.

Poor Rachel hardly knew which way to turn. Apart from overseeing the arrival of the furniture, she had to feed us, organise the house and, almost immediately, see about getting Tristan ready for his new school. We all agreed that the sooner he got started the better it would be and he was as keen as anyone to get on with it.

Some time before we left England I had searched through a number of advertisements for a builder. The man I found lived some way off and after he had given us a couple of references we agreed that he should come over soon after our arrival and see what had to be done. He was due to come over any day now and, whilst waiting for him, we had our first big shock. I was standing in the kitchen when I heard Rachel cry out 'Drains!' She was standing at the back door leading into the courtyard wearing that particular expression of hers which spells trouble.

'Drains', she cried again. 'Can't you smell them?' I had to admit that, without any doubt, there was that dreadful all-pervading smell which means only one thing – serious problems down below. A search of the courtyard revealed the two miscreant *fosses septiques*. One had collapsed completely and was responsible for the ghastly smell and the other looked as though it was well on its way.

This was one of our first challenges and we picked up the phone book, wondering where we might find those worthies whose livelihoods depend on drains like ours. Within a couple of days our first French artisans appeared to study the matter, gave us their considered opinions and presented us with the estimates for curing the ills.

Whilst all this was going on our British builder duly appeared. He was a great brute of a fellow, built like an ox and had a lazy eye. I always find this a trifle unsettling and throughout the time he was with us I could never remember which one to look into, invariably finding myself looking into the wrong eye when we were talking. He had with him his assistant and the three of us toured the property looking at what I wanted them to do. I told him that we had just six months of the new year to sort out the initial batch of problems after which we would have to stop as we would be expecting visitors.

Without a moment's hesitation he gave us the first of his many problems announcing that he would not be able to start for some time. He followed this by highlighting the difficulties he would have driving over each day and we suggested they should stay with us during the week and leave at weekends. He then announced that he had very few tools and we would need to go and hire most of the things he needed. Once more my antennae sensed problems ahead but by now we were committed.

Another *fosse septique* expert then appeared to inspect our drains. Monsieur Rigal told us that he did not understand why we had called the others in to have a look. He was a Massac man and this was his patch, furthermore he could do our drains quicker and more cheaply than the others. He produced his credentials, lit a filthy cigarette, and told us that we could come and see his work if we so wished.

We declined this invitation telling him that we were fully convinced of his abilities and agreed to engage him. He was an extraordinary character, short and immensely powerfully built, and with little or no neck he at once reminded us of James Bond's adversary – Odd Job – all he needed was my bowler hat.

At seven one morning later that week we heard the sound of engines. It was Odd Job, cigarette dangling from a corner of his mouth, leading a small convoy of a JCB, a small van and a lorry loaded with all manner of drains and pipes. With great authority and much arm waving he announced that he was going to cut all the drain outlets where they emerged from the house and then redo the whole outside network of drains linking them all to one enormous *fosse septique*, the outlet of which would finish up somewhere in the ditch the far side of the orchard. He assured us that we need not worry. Essential services, he announced with a chuckle, would be maintained throughout. '*Pas de problème*, Mooseur King!'

Within a couple of hours the courtyard resembled the battle of the Somme. Deep channels and mountains of earth everywhere, the place looked doomed. Outside the road was taken up to lay the drains and from there it all disappeared off somewhere into the ditch. It took just three days and it was a remarkable piece of work. Archie and Sarah had told us that the quality of work in France was superb so long as one did not engage cowboys.

Just before Christmas we had our first local visitors. About a mile down the valley there is a very attractive house set back into the northern side of the valley with a marvellous southerly aspect. We often wondered who lived there and now here they all were on our doorstep. Jonathan Bell, a tall, quietly spoken American introduced himself and his wife Marie-Claire. She was locally born, knew the locality and local community inside out and spoke perfect English.

It was a wonderful surprise and they were a great help in the months ahead as we battled away to get ourselves sorted out. They and their two sons live here for most of the year but try to get back to the States for the long summer holidays. Jonathan, a freelance journalist, is often away on business but we have become good friends and frequently spend evenings together putting the world straight.

Christmas came and went but not before we had been asked to drive over to the Shaws for a New Year's Eve party. We had an early lunch before setting out and in the middle of it all there was a sharp crack. Rachel and Tristan looked across at me. Horror of horrors, a particularly resistant piece of French bread had destroyed my upper dentures which had snapped clean in half. I felt and looked like a toothless old peasant and steadfastly refused to present myself at the Shaws' smart New Year's Eve party in that condition, evening dress or not. Out came the phone book in a desperate attempt to find a dentist open on New Year's Eve with a skilled technician hanging around waiting for someone to appear with broken dentures.

Our first call was to a number in Lavaur where the cheerful receptionist told me to come in right away and they would see what could be done. They were quite brilliant. There was indeed a technician there and he reassembled the bits in my mouth much to the amusement of the two pert little assistants.

'No problem,' he announced, 'Can you come back in an hour and a half?' In a remarkable demonstration of prompt and efficient service I was fitted out with my smartly reinforced upper set and off we went to enjoy a memorable evening with Archie and Sarah.

After a splendid New Year's Eve party we returned to face the tasks that lay ahead. Our builder returned early in the New Year and began to toil away but the red warning lights got ever brighter as time wore on. He seemed quite out of his depth with everything we asked him to do. What he achieved was not done badly but he was falling way behind even his pessimistic schedule.

At last he was out of the house and into the *gîte* but here things got slower and worse, culminating in him having an accident on his way here. This threw his schedule completely. We had not yet reached the panic stage but time was marching on and we had to meet our deadline. We cast around for other builders but the local French firms had their hands full and I was put on to another British builder – against our better judgment and the Shaws' advice – but there was nobody else.

\* \* \*

The leader of the team came over from Gaillac where he lived and saw what had to be done. Harry, an affable and self-assured character, had been in the house renovation business out here for a number of years and had assembled a small team around him. Comments on his work were, at this time, not unfavourable and I asked him if he could do what had to be done in the time we had left. He looked at me and said with all the confidence in the world that it would be done and that he would let me know how things were progressing.

As soon as I heard this I decided to change horses and confronted our original builder telling him that we could not continue in this fashion and that he would have to go. I never find this easy but there was no option and they went on their way, the new team arriving almost immediately. Harry asked me for a substantial amount of money in advance so he could pay his team. A week later he asked for more and soon after that for a third payment in advance – all in cash.

Once again we were beginning to feel uncomfortable but our hands were tied and we had to press on. A short time later he came to say that he was going to have to revise his estimate upwards by some 25 per cent as they had come across a number of problems. Two weeks later there was another increase – his original estimate had now all but doubled.

Over dinner one evening I confessed to Rachel that I was feeling uneasy about this new lot and that we were being steamrollered. They too were getting behindhand, sometimes just one man was here on his own, on other occasions nobody turned up. The work was being left in the most dreadful state at the end of the day, Harry often just walking off the site through a pile of dust and rubble left on the floor, leaving a trail of debris behind him as he walked down the stairs and out of the front door.

More and more excuses for delays until I asked Harry which of the jobs that we had agreed originally, and for which he had given us an estimate, would not be finished in time. I was stunned by his reply when he told me, quite casually, that several jobs would not be finished, others not even attempted. Had I handed over any more money I would have paid him for everything we had discussed, whether they had done it or not. It was a bitter blow and I realised that we would not be ready in time. Our plans were in a mess.

By now we had grown to know a number of French people and through them and the Bells I found out the names of artisans who would be able to finish Harry's work. They came and gave their estimates just before Harry and his team left. The inevitable moment came when he asked if we could settle up, and do so as quickly as possible for he had other business to attend to and wanted to be on his way.

I invited him into the study, asked him to sit down and got him to confirm that he was now expecting to be paid in full for everything we had agreed to at our first meeting. He assured me he was.

'Well that's fine,' I said. 'However I am afraid to say that our figures don't quite match.' I produced the paper that had all the original work written down and went through the list highlighting the jobs that had not been started and for which he had just confirmed that he was expecting payment.

The room was very quiet. Harry had been hoisted by his own petard and well he knew it. I reminded him that he had assured me everything would be finished in time and told him that, seeing this coming, I had got estimates for all the outstanding work. These I intended to deduct from the figure he had in mind and pay him the balance.

'Just pay me whatever you think fit,' he said, not looking at me.

'No Harry, I am not going to do that. I am going to pay you in full for everything you have done but I am not paying you anything for work you haven't done. Let there be no misunderstanding about this, you are being properly paid for work done.'

Harry had made a brazen and clumsy effort to coerce me, the new boy, into paying more than was due. It was pretty unimpressive, nothing short of cavalier and we had been let down badly. We went our separate ways and later word filtered back that a good yarn had been spun about us. It is a sorry little tale which brought home to us the less attractive side of the British community. Had we been able to go elsewhere we surely would have done but the spectre of Black Monday, the ERM and the crash of the Pound was beginning to haunt us.

We were now due to put the swimming pool into the lower orchard and had engaged a bona fide British firm to install an American pool which appealed to us. Odd Job reappeared, this time with a huge machine that trundled slowly up through the orchard, the very trees shaking as it passed by. We had decided to put in a large amount of terracing around the pool as we hoped that a fair number of people might be using it at any one time and we did not want them to be heaped on top of one another.

In addition we had chosen to dig the whole pool complex down so that all the terracing would be on terra firma rather than one side having to be banked up and then supported with retaining walls. Again huge mountains of earth were displaced as Odd Job did his work superbly, cutting the shape of the pool to within an inch or so.

The pool team stayed with us for the ten days it took to do the work and left us with a very smart new pool in the middle of a muddy waste that now had to be landscaped. Odd Job knew of a retired man who was, so he assured us, a superb artisan who we should engage to do the terracing. Nodding vigorously and, as if to emphasise the point, he removed the ever-present cigarette, blew a big kiss into the wind and threw his arms wide.

Monsieur Ricard, a delightful little man, well into his sixties appeared, had a good look at what was wanted and announced that he would do it. It would take a month but we would be satisfied with the result. Slowly but surely the terracing took shape around the pool and a few days before it was finished we filled the pool and Tristan broke the ice.

Soon after, while we were working in the garden, we heard a commotion from the pool and sounds of shouting. We rushed to the scene and found a sodden, bedraggled and very shocked Monsieur

Ricard. He explained that, whilst taking one of the large and very heavy paving tiles across the terrace, he had tripped and fallen into the pool. By the grace of God the extremely heavy tile had gone in first; had the unfortunate Monsieur Ricard gone in first and the tile crashed on top of him we would now be waiting for the hearse.

The brand new liner had taken the full force of the tile and had been split. Then, as Monsieur Ricard tried to get the tile out, it had ripped the liner in a number of other places. The poor man was distraught and we took him into the house to dry out and regain his composure while Tristan and I spent a difficult hour or so attempting to identify and patch the cuts and tears.

Monsieur Ricard duly completed a superb job as Odd Job had promised and we engaged him to do a bit more tiling for us in the house. When we came to settle the second account he refused to take a centime, his parting words to us being '*Seulement un petit cadeau!*'

As if all this was not enough Rachel had decided that the wiring in the main house was ancient, unstable and positively dangerous – every bit of it needed to be replaced. The existing wires were fixed to the walls but the new wires were, she insisted, to go into the walls. This meant that every wall in the house had to be attacked with jack hammers, the wires laid in the grooves and the walls resealed.

We were given the name of an electrician in Lavaur and Monsieur Osbini came out to introduce himself and examine our electrics. He set about his work briskly, moving quickly from room to room making copious notes, all the while smiling and chatting away, jumping up to inspect this or bending down to check that. Blessed with a quick wit he was never short of a joke or a smile.

He and his small team set about their work with an impressive professionalism. Although the noise was deafening and the dust something of a nightmare we were never without power and at the end of each day Monsieur Osbini set his team to clearing up what of the mess they could. When I came to settle up with him we found that he was ahead of schedule and he showed me a number of places where he had been able to save us some money. Needless to say he has remained firmly on our books as has the good Odd Job.

Back in the depths of winter I realised that we would have to produce some literature and start advertising if we were going to catch any customers at all for the following summer. The Shaws had given us some good advice but now it was time to put pen to paper. Producing a leaflet was going to be difficult. I needed some good photos of the house (it was now mid-winter), of the rooms (they all had to be redecorated) and, of course, the pool which, at that point, was nothing more than a rectangle of tape in the orchard.

When we had paid our last visit back in the summer I had taken some photos of the house, a couple of which had turned out rather well and we had another shot of the cottage. These, together with a map of the area, made up the visual display on our first leaflet and, together, we extolled the virtues of Bosc Lebat and this corner of France as best we could.

Jonathan – our *immobilier* – was still living in Toulouse and he put me in touch with a printing firm in the student quarter of the city. The lovely Madame Salmon listened patiently to our requirements and ran off a proof copy that we liked. Now we were really on our way and we followed this with a run of advertisements in a number of holiday magazines.

It was now very late in the year to start this sort of thing and we only just caught the tail end of the advertising season. However a number of enquiries eventually drifted in and when our first bookings were confirmed we had the names of our first guests and an actual date by which we had to be ready.

We had done all we could in the time available to get the house, the cottage and the grounds ready. Now it was simply a matter of preparing ourselves to receive boarders. Literally that!

# CHAPTER VII

# *The Flag is Raised*

*In and around the house. The piano disaster. Some early entertaining. Making our furniture. Good advice and good beds.*

Once we had moved in, unpacked and settled we began to get a feel for the place. Bosc Lebat, like any other substantial house, had some parts in better condition than others. Although large it has well proportioned south-facing rooms and stands on its own, secluded and surrounded by the gardens and grounds. However, it is not an intimidating house and the three of us are always happy here on our own. The large generous windows give the house plenty of light and in the summer the rooms remain lit by the evening sun until late.

We arrived to find that the large room to the right of the front door was a shambles. It had been left by the previous owners as something of a glory hole into which everything that had not got a proper home was thrown and forgotten. The old tiled floor was in a sorry state, the walls a mess and a plasterboard partition divided the room into two. However there were lights, plugs and a telephone point so we decided to set up a temporary office here while we tackled the rest of the house, leaving this room – later to become our drawing room – until last.

We decided also to store Rachel's lovely Bechstein Grand piano in there until we found a permanent home elsewhere. We covered it well to keep off the worst of the dust created by Monsieur Osbini and his merry men as they rewired the house and kept the room as dry as possible. Some time in the spring Rachel felt she could wait no longer and went to have a look at her piano. She took off the wraps and tried to play but it was a disaster. Some notes were way off key whilst others stuck – something had gone badly, horribly wrong.

We had been told about an excellent piano tuner in Castres, a large town some twenty miles away near the Black Mountains. The good Monsieur Parisot was contacted and came over to inspect the mess, stripping the piano down to see what was amiss. It did not take him long and he came into the kitchen with a grave look on his face.

'Come and look at this,' he said. We followed him back to the piano and gathered round to see what he had found. He put his hand inside and drew it back again – it was wringing wet.

'This is bad news, I'm afraid to say. Very bad news. I fear that some damage has been done, perhaps even some serious damage. You will have to move it out of here quickly or you will lose it.' Rachel was distraught. This was her pride and joy, something with which she could lose herself and play for hour after hour whenever she wanted to escape from the world. But, as Monsieur Parisot had announced, the piano was now very sick, the damage done and it needed to be taken away for major repairs.

Thankfully Monsieur Parisot was as good as his reputation and for several months he worked on the piano, sending the most complicated pieces away to Germany to be reworked. Eventually it came back, as good as new, and now lives in the room to the left of the front door which we use as the music room. The room in which the piano so nearly died was left closed down for a while but it is now fully restored.

When the three of us are alone together we eat in the kitchen, leaving the dining room for special occasions or when there a number of guests. The kitchen is warmed by a large wood-burning stove that doubles as a hotplate as Rachel prepares the evening meals and if we have just a couple of visitors we ask them to join us there. It is a cosy place on a dark winter's evening and often we remain at the table long after the meal has finished, passing around a large basket of walnuts and bottle of wine.

'Monsieur Parisot stripped the piano to see what was amiss.'

Once the weather is warmer we have our meals outside whenever we can, either on the terrace just outside the kitchen or on the long rustic table under the chestnuts on the top lawn. Again we like to remain sitting at the table after the meal listening to the birds and crickets as the day draws to a close. Sometimes Rachel will slip away into the music room and play, the soft notes of the piano drifting across the garden to where the guests sit in silence taking in the peace and quiet of the surroundings.

We knew that we had come to live in an area of France famous for its wonderful food, each area boasting its own great menus. Rachel is an excellent cook and has learned many of the local recipes which she is happy to introduce to our guests. However, when we invite our French friends in for dinner they like to sample English cooking and we have our favourites which are always popular. In spite of my modest efforts at French we all enjoy the evenings when our neighbours come to join us. Sometimes it is just our French friends, sometimes a mixture and, on occasions, a veritable Tower of Babel – but always fun.

One day early in our first summer, Jamie was helping me prepare the *gîte* for our first visitors. As he was tidying the small log shed a car drew up with three young French people inside. The driver, a woman, asked him if this was where there was a *gîte* to let. Although she spoke excellent English, Jamie brought her over to the house and we met Eliane, one of our near neighbours, for the first time. After some discussion the couple with her arranged to take the *gîte* for the winter and we got talking to Eliane about the area.

She and her friend, Jean, have a lovely home just over the hill to our east, set in a marvellous position with panoramic views across to the Black Mountains and Pyrenees. Both work in Toulouse where they have become deeply involved with the commercial activities of the city. Eliane's job entails a great deal of travelling, in particular to the UK. Bright, quick witted and with a great sense of humour Eliane is a tireless bundle of energy and has her finger firmly on the pulse of Toulouse.

Through her we began to appreciate just what a dynamic city it has become – yet again we were thankful for having decided to come and live here.

Marc and Pascale – friend's of Eliane's – duly moved in during the autumn and were well settled by winter time. They were a delightful couple and, come Christmas, we decided to go all the way with the great meals, agreeing that they would entertain us for the traditional French celebration on Christmas Eve and we would be at home to them and their parents the following day – with lots of exercise in between.

Rachel decided to do an evening meal in the best of British tradition and at some point in the afternoon the oven was heated and the turkey began its last journey. Everything was timed to the last minute and we had decided to dress for the occasion, opening the evening's proceedings with champagne in the drawing room. A few minutes before our guests appeared Rachel went to see how the turkey was behaving. I hovered near the front door waiting for the knock on the door when the most awful howl came from the kitchen.

Fearing the worst I dashed to the point of the drama and found the lady of the house on hands and knees. The turkey and roast potatoes, together with gravy, trimmings and everything else to do with it, had absented itself from the plate and crashed to the floor. If this was not enough the dogs, sensing a free-for-all, had appeared in the doorway. We leapt at the fearful mess and, after much scrummaging around, a lot of giggling, and some very bad language, regained the initiative.

The wretched bird, together with all the attendant bits and pieces, was replated, everything else arranged neatly around it and the whole lot shoved back into the oven to do its damnest. A large glass of bubbly calmed the nerves, a second restored morale and our feet were back on the ground once more. As if on cue, the door knocker crashed and the show was on the road.

Lest sharp eyes at the table should detect that anything was amiss, I boosted the champagne into a powerful cocktail and kept up a full flow until dinner was served. By this stage they were ready for anything, airborne turkeys included and, come the end of the meal, rose up to toast the chef for her efforts.

Although still early days, we loved entertaining and would find any excuse for a dinner party or Sunday lunch. Language was rarely a problem and, on occasions, a little stumble with the finer points of another tongue would lift the roof. We had met a delightful couple from Mazamet and invited them over to meet some of our other friends. Max and Nicole were very positive and always great fun – he spoke good English whilst Nicole, though not quiet so fluent, made up for it by just launching herself at the problem. Lunch had begun, we were well into the main course and the conversation around the table was getting noisy. Nicole was sitting on my left chatting away when suddenly she decided to take centre stage.

'Fuck!' she yelled. Immediately the room fell silent, not a movement anywhere, knives, forks and glasses held motionless. 'Yes, fuck! It's beautiful!' Nicole now had the room's complete and undivided attention; everyone staring down the table wide-eyed in anticipation at what might come next. 'I love your English. I want Rachel to teach me all the good words and Paddy to show me all the very naughty ones.'

I glanced up and noticed that this little gem – all ten seconds of it – had caused the last drop of wine to be drained from every glass on the table. Rising to play the good host I said quietly to Nicole, now laughing quite uproariously, that if I was ever to show her these things, I would have to seek permission from the one at the other end of the table, and that might be a bit difficult.

The principal rooms at Bosc Lebat are set at the front of the house and behind are the usual humble rooms of domestic necessity. Our decision to use the bedroom suite downstairs ourselves meant that the main upstairs bedroom area was left to the guests and our four sons who have their own wing. Sadly they are not here often but when they do come for a break it is nice for them to have their own corner of the house.

We knocked the place around as little as possible as time was short and we had a mass of things to renovate and redecorate. However, additions had to be made to the plumbing here and there, both upstairs and down. Last but not least, beyond the study and across the back hall, there is the old cold room which we converted into a downstairs cloakroom. Rachel refuses to use the place: not only does it remain by far the coldest room in the house, but the walls are festooned with my old military photographs. That, she claims, is no place for a lady with half the British Army grinning at you or glaring angrily at whatever is going on.

The windows at the back of the house look out across a delightful old courtyard which in times gone by was, no doubt, the centre of activities at Bosc Lebat. On the far side is the old Guardian's House – now known simply as the *gîte* – and next to this is the old *pigeonnier*. Built in mellowed brick with its own tiled roof it is an attractive building with a dozen pigeon holes arranged close together under the roof.

The doves, now long since gone, have been replaced by our friends the barn owls. If we sit quietly at the back of the house at dusk we often catch sight of the birds as they emerge from their front door and take to the evening air. Some years they nest up there and, early in the summer, we watch enthralled as the young owlets take up their positions in the little pigeon holes waiting for their parents to swoop down with supper. Owl watch is always a popular time.

To the left of the *pigeonnier* are the great four-metre-high doors to the courtyard set in front of the large archway through which the horses or oxen would pull carts of wood or produce for the household. Beyond the arch is the old forge where the farrier used to shoe the horses and oxen of the *manoir* as well as those from many other farms in the neighbourhood.

It is not difficult to imagine the place, perhaps until just a few years ago, being the centre of local gossip as the farmhands from nearby farms and homesteads chatted away while waiting for their beasts to be shod. It is an empty building now but the great fireplace is still there as are the farrier's quarters next door. Beyond that again is a row of small buildings

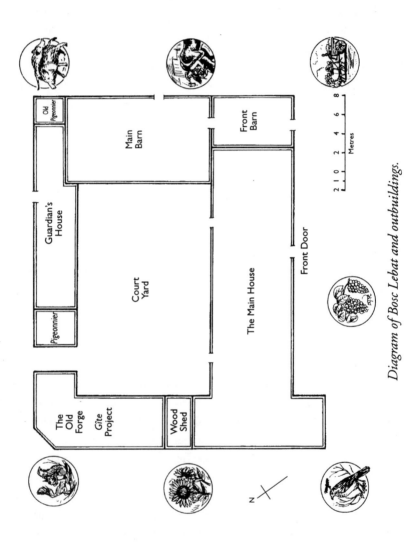

*Diagram of Bosc Lebat and outbuildings.*

where poultry, rabbits and goats for the house were kept, together with the dogs.

The right-hand side of the courtyard is taken up by a wall of the great barn. In the far corner of the yard is one of the deep original wells and, throughout the time we have been at Bosc Lebat, it has never run dry. The courtyard itself is an area of gravel and grass in the middle of which there is a large lilac together with a very old blue hibiscus. Creepers and wild roses climb the walls of the *gîte* and barn, providing a haven for small birds. What was once a place full of bustle and activity is now one of peace and quiet. It is a beautiful spot, one of my favourite corners of Bosc Lebat.

That was the house as we found it. If it was going to suit our purposes there was a great deal to be done. Not so much with the hammer and saw (although quite enough of that) but, painting, decorating, making the curtains and, of course, furnishing the rooms. We had come with the contents of two houses but we had two houses to furnish here, added to which, one was a big house with big rooms in which most of our furniture, made to fit into small English houses, looked ridiculous. Furniture is expensive and we needed a good deal of it so we set about buying it in bit by bit.

In days gone by up to fifty cattle were wintered in the great barn. The old stalls are still there, as is the cowman's room halfway up the stairs to the loft. It is a cosy little room and one can well imagine him living here above his charges, one ear cocked towards the rattle of the cow chains and the gentle calling of the beasts, he and his room kept warm by the heat of the cattle below. Hay and fodder were once stored in the huge loft above the cow barn and one day, when poking around up there, I came across a large stack of timber. The planks were cut neatly into lengths and laid out tidily on pegs to avoid warping as the wood seasoned.

The timber looked to be in good condition and I wondered if we would be able to use any of it to make furniture for the house. We had heard of a retired carpenter who was adept at making furniture to whatever specifications were required, so, one evening, I rang him and explained what we had found. I told him that we needed a number of pieces made up and that we had some timber he might be able to use.

Monsieur Calmet came out and we showed him what we wanted and where it was to go. Once in the dining room he asked the two of us to pull up chairs and sit where we thought the ends of the table should be. He then took measurements around us, all the while discussing how high and wide the piece should be in keeping with the room, the depth of the top and the shape of the base – as a tailor might measure a customer for a new suit.

It would be no problem he assured us but warned that seasoned oak of the quantity and quality we required came at a high price. We took him round the house showing him where we needed other pieces – a large coffee table, a very big bookcase and a blanket chest for the upstairs landing before going outside and up into the loft over the barn.

The old man knelt beside the large pile of wood as his son, Daniel, moved the planks this way and that for him to see in the light. The first two layers were of seasoned oak and of a quality that impressed the artisan.

Suddenly he gave a cry, 'Elm, *mon Dieu*,' then 'And look at this – cherry and walnut.' Plank after plank of these rare and valuable woods were brought out and the old craftsman rubbed his hands gently along the grain enthusing about the quality of the wood.

I thought we might have a bargain for I could do nothing with timber of this quality whilst to the old man it was pure gold. In the end we came to a deal which was for him to take the rare timber and in return he would make us our furniture. Six weeks later the ancient van came spluttering around the corner with our furniture on board, the back doors open with various pieces protruding, everything being held in place by Daniel and his girlfriend. He completed the assembly of the table in the dining room and announced with pride that if thieves

'The old man knelt by the large pile of wood.'

wanted it they would have to carry away almost 250 kilos of solid oak table.

Not only had he made a table to our exact specifications but in perfect harmony with the room itself. Just how much a heavy oak table such as this, one which can seat a dozen with comfort, would have cost us we shuddered to think. Monsieur Calmet is a great craftsman and as the other pieces were taken into the various rooms each space was filled perfectly. It was our first windfall at Bosc Lebat and we reckoned it was about time that Lady Luck had graced us with her presence.

'There are only three things you need to worry about in your doss house,' cried an old and worldly friend of mine before we left England.

'Seriously comfortable beds, crisp fresh linen and unlimited hot water. Give them that and they'll be happy as cows in the corn. If you don't there will be hell to pay. Take my word for it – happy holidaymakers will get home and tell a couple of chums about their visit but one grumpy old sod who couldn't sleep will bang on all winter about it, telling the world, his wife and anybody else he can find, not to touch the place with a bargepole. A few like that and you'll be in deep trouble.'

Needless to say beds were next on our list for, yet again, we found that our small beds from home were just not big enough to suit all comers. We drove over to Castres where Rachel had found some very large, expensive, orthopaedically designed beds in a sale. There were no frills about them such as ornamental headboards or other bits and pieces. They were just very large, firm beds that could be either one enormous double (room enough for peace or war) or separated into two spacious singles.

Not built as things of beauty, their sole purpose in life was to ensure that those on board got a good night's sleep and they were just about the best buy we made. Not once in the years we have been here have any guests come down to breakfast grumbling about not being able to get to sleep and that includes men up to six feet eight inches tall and another that weighed in at almost twenty stones.

In fact, so comfy are the beds that, on one occasion, a couple flew in from London to spend a long weekend with us. They arrived late and the following morning we hung around for ages waiting for them to put in an appearance. We had all but given up hope of seeing them for breakfast when suddenly, and with much theatre, the good lady appeared clad in her negligée, hair akimbo: a wild look about her – like Lady Macbeth.

'My God,' she cried, 'your beds really are comfy. I've just come down for a bit of fruit, do you mind? We're nesting hard up there and won't be down for a bit – don't worry about us and forget the breakfast.' With that she leapt away upstairs, desperate to regain her bed and get on with whatever it was that required more fruit.

Life, in those early days was rarely, if ever dull.

# CHAPTER VIII

# Settling Down

*The garden and grounds. Tristan – school and social life.*
*Rugby in France.*

Rachel and I had decided that she would be responsible for all that
went on inside the house and *gîte* whilst I had to look after the
roofs, guttering, outside walls and everything else outside. It was an even
distribution of responsibilities and saved us from getting into a tangle
over this or that. We had bought Bosc Lebat with fifteen acres of
gardens, orchards, paddocks and woods on which there were a number
of outbuildings so I was going to be busy.

As all this was my domain, it was up to me to get on with it as best as
I could. I tended to leave the buildings well alone until something fell
off or broke but the gardens required constant attention. The front door
opens on to a long narrow terrace that runs the length of the house
beyond which is the front drive. Beyond this again is the top lawn where
there are some of the lovely trees that abound on the property, in
particular the line of chestnuts that gives us shade from the summer heat
and an enormous lime whose heady fragrance attracts myriads of
butterflies and bees in the summer.

Before we left England a rose grower from the Midlands had heard
about our plans and asked if we would like to set up a rose garden of
English roses. Nothing could have been nicer and soon after our arrival,
Bernard, our postman struggled in with no less than two hundred plants
ready for the garden. They had to go in right away thus all other

activities were suspended whilst the beds were hastily prepared and the roses from England introduced to the soil of France, many of them along the front of the top lawn.

To the right of the lawn is the summer house and underneath is the old fruit and cider store. We have put a small water feature against the summer house wall. It is a simple little affair of water tumbling from a lion's mouth into two small pools where I have put some miniature irises and other aquatic plants. The sound of gently falling water is pleasantly relaxing for those sitting in deck chairs under the chestnuts or resting in the guest rooms.

Beyond the top lawn the garden falls away to the main orchard where we put the pool. It is only fifty yards from the front door but out of sight behind a hedge and beneath the beautiful old coach house that is now our garage. We have around sixty trees in the orchards, more than half of them young walnuts. The remainder are fruit trees of every kind, keeping us well supplied throughout the summer and from which Rachel makes mountains of chutney and jam.

On the far side of the orchard and the swimming pool is the second of our fields and the large, eight-acre wood. Here, deep in the wood and high up in the tree tops, lives a colony of delightful little red squirrels. We see them often, scampering across the lawns about their business, a wary eye open for the dogs.

Wild boar continue to rest up in the wood during their autumn and spring migrations, buzzards nest at the far end and all around in the thickets nightingales and warblers set up their homes on their return in the spring. It is a wonderful haven of wildlife. We leave it well alone and have cut just one circuit of paths up through the wood so that our visitors can stroll up there and listen to the natural world around them.

I try to manage the grounds myself but from time to time have to call in extra help to deal with the ditches and rough corners. The previous owners had given me the name of the old pensioner who used to help them out and I called Monsieur Peche asking him up to discuss business. I heard the little *mobilette* long before I caught sight of it. The tiny motor was straining for all its worth as it bore the considerable bulk of Monsieur Peche and his hedging tools up the valley road towards the house. He pulled up by the great barn where, I strongly suspect, he had done for years. Slowly and very deliberately he dismounted, took off his ancient helmet and blinked at me in the bright sunlight.

'Uh,' he cried loudly, 'Uh, *Bonjour Monsieur, bonjour.*' We looked at each other and his face broke into a wide, warm smile. We shook hands and his enormous, powerful hand closed over mine, pressing just hard enough to let me know that there was an awful lot more power there. I introduced myself and explained what my request for help was all about. He never took his twinkling eyes away from mine and heard me out save for the occasional loud 'Uh!' To this day I believe that all I needed to have said was 'Monsieur Peche – same game, same rules. *Allez y!*'

He knew exactly what was required of him and set to work at a formidable rate, beginning at dawn and working non-stop through the morning until noon. At this point his day was done and I used to hear the little motor taking him off to Madame Peche for *le grand repas.*

The good man had nearly twenty years on me but went through the undergrowth at a rate I could only marvel at. Hands and feet as hard as nails, he used to work in the wet ditches barefoot, the brambles, nettles and thorn making no impact on the leather hide. Once I watched him work as he passed a wasps' nest, the angry insects flying at their opponent in wave after wave. A heavy swat with the hand and the inevitable 'Uh!' were the only signs that one had found its target. When I could get him to stop he would tell me about life at Bosc Lebat before the War when the house was full of servants and the land was tilled by horse and ox. He would recount tales of terrible weather like all old country folk do.

'You want to look out for the *vent d'autan*,' he warned, referring to the fierce gale that sometimes blows in from the mountains and can last for days like the Mistral. 'All right down here under the oaks but you wouldn't want to be up on the ridge. Can be terrible sometimes, takes roofs off, drives men mad.' The mere idea of it made the old fellow shake with laughter.

Then, with a chuckle he added, 'Napoleon had it right, you know. Understood these things, he did. If a man killed his wife whilst the *vent d'autan* was blowing, he was excused – let off. That Napoleon! Knew what was what he did. 'Twas the women that drove the men mad, you know – not the wind. He knew that but he was one of the boys, he was.' I always enjoy Monsieur Peche's presence around the place and, at the end of each season, we have a quick *vin d'honneur* to put the year to bed and get ready for the next.

Behind the house and beyond the courtyard the *gîte* has its own garden and beyond this again is the big wood barn. Until the arrival of the central heating system Bosc Lebat had used only wood as fuel for heating the house and, luckily for us, we have more than enough.

One of the few things our predecessors had failed to do was to keep the woods well tended and over the years the young oaks had proliferated until they had become hopelessly overgrown and badly needed to be culled. This was to be a serious undertaking for even a young oak is a massive piece of timber and has to be treated with respect when it is being felled. Yet again I turned to our neighbours to get myself out of a dilemma.

Nearby, in the next village, lives a large family called Gaillard who burn wood for all their needs – cooking as well as heating. They are always on the lookout for timber and one day when I met Monsieur Gaillard at the Saturday market I put it to him that a deal might be arranged. He would clear our woods stage by stage, fell the surplus timber, take some for himself and put the remainder in my barn. A few days later he appeared at the house and together we walked the course looking at the trees deciding which ones should go and which should be kept.

A deal was struck as to who would have how much and he returned with a couple of friends and set to work. They did a marvellous job, first clearing the undergrowth, then felling the trees. After this they stripped off the brushwood, then sawed the trunks and limbs into lengths before splitting and stacking them. It was hard work indeed and although I have been accused of giving them too good a deal, whenever I see them up there in the depths of winter, stripped to the waist and sweating away I know that it has been a fair bargain.

I, too, have my part to play in bringing the wood to the fire for, once the wood is in the wood barn, I have to saw the timber into lengths. These I then split with the axe and carry them from there to the courtyard where they are stacked again before making their final journey to the fire. Seasoned oak is heavy, as anyone who has helped me on these chores appreciates, and nobody puts on weight in the wood barn.

The road that winds its way up to Bosc Lebat from Massac is hardly more than a lane. It passes the house and *gîte* before climbing up the hill behind where it joins another busier road. Very little traffic uses the valley, in fact most people think it is our own road and stop at the bottom of our drive before retracing their steps. It is a pretty little road, winding its way through the fields, passing just a couple of houses before it reaches the village.

There is another way down the valley and that is the old carter's track that follows the stream along the bottom, running parallel to the road before meeting up with it this side of the village. The two routes make a lovely walk and if we do come across a vehicle it is usually one of our neighbours and there is always time for a chat about the weather, the crops, the *chasse* or other country matters.

Those who farm the land around us and the people who live here have come to know us. As in rural areas everywhere the presence of newcomers or strangers is noticed at once but it takes a long time before friendships are struck up. In the first few months we had little time to meet our neighbours apart from Jonathan and Marie-Clare but, as time went on, we have got to know the lie of the land and who lives where.

Tristan had been at his new school since early November. Starting a new school anywhere is daunting enough but when you are the only new face and a foreigner as well it is especially testing. In his case Tristan was not only the subject of much curiosity as he was English but there was the small matter of language that attracted attention. It was easy enough for him to study his French back in Winchester when a delightful elderly lady took the time and trouble to help him on his way but out here it was quite another matter.

His contemporaries would be chattering away nineteen to the dozen, totally indifferent to his existence and, as all youngsters do, would have the occasional laugh at his expense as he tried to join the conversation. Add to this the thick rolling burr of the south-west together with all the nuances, insinuations and slang of a foreign language, the whole lot going at a hundred kilometres per hour, and the size of the problem facing the lad becomes apparent.

But that was just the social side of it all – on the bus, in the dining hall and outside the classroom. Inside the classroom it became serious stuff as the mysteries of physics and chemistry were unravelled, as were French, history, geography, maths, sociology and philosophy. And if all this was not bad enough there was Latin and Spanish to be mastered in French by the young lad from England – all those supine stems, gerundives, adjectival clauses and heaven knows what else.

An additional problem for him was to adjust to the differences between working for the *baccalauréat* here in France as opposed towards his GCSEs and A Levels in England. Until the end of College (roughly equivalent to Secondary school) both systems are very similar in that the students advance on a broad front taking ten or a dozen subjects. Once past this stage youngsters in the UK concentrate on reading just three or four subjects for A level, the results of which determine whether or not university will follow.

The French *baccalauréat* demands that ten or more subjects are maintained throughout the time at the *lycée*. The pressure is remorseless, in particular where students such as Tristan had to absorb everything in a foreign language. Funnily enough, when it was all over and we had time to reflect on the two systems, we felt that both were flawed – the

British system is too narrow and too deep, whilst the French one demands, what appeared to us, an unnecessary breadth of knowledge at this level.

A sensible compromise on both sides of the Channel might be for the students to study five or six subjects in depth whilst maintaining the basic skills in the parent language and simple mathematics – the good old Three Rs whose demise is bemoaned by teaching staff in France just as much as it is by those in the UK.

It was a very tall order for Tristan, but, to his eternal credit, he stuck to his guns and slowly but surely got on level terms with his classmates. He made progress and on occasions he even came top of the class. We were proud of him and mightily relieved for, had he not been able to cope, we would have been in a dreadful fix. Tristan, like all of us, had his moments of despair, and from time to time any one of us could feel exhausted, depressed and overcome by the enormity of it all.

We got around the dangers of open warfare by agreeing that, on these particular occasions, whoever felt like this was allowed to vent their angst and frustration on the rest of us. It was the duty of the remainder to bite on the bullet, offer some sympathy and support but never to return the fire so that we would all end up yelling and screaming. It seemed to work and in those early hectic months we all took strength and comfort from each other when the going got rough and this helped to keep things moving ahead smoothly.

Gradually Tristan's social life came together and friends would appear at the house, sometimes to join us for a meal or to disappear off upstairs to his rooms with a pack of beer. We were delighted to see that his friends came from all corners – sometimes members of the rugby team, sometimes chums from the *lycée* and sometimes sons of our friends.

We let him get on with his life as much as possible but inevitably he was caught up with our guests when we had dinner together. Even in the beginning he found that he had an interesting tale to tell and was often quizzed closely on the differences in the education systems or the rugby scene or the attitude of the French young to this or that. He learned quickly how to cope with difficult or inane questions, how to handle a delicate topic and how to give a balanced view on a variety of subjects. Initially it was quite difficult for him but in a very short time he learned to be at ease with his elders and it was a fruitful introduction to what might lie ahead in discussions at university or job interviews.

On his last summer with us he decided to go off hitch-hiking alone around Europe. Rachel was unsure about this but I helped plan his trip, get his equipment together and gave him a few tips about hitch-hiking, explaining what motorists looked for when they came across someone at the side of the road. Scruffy, unwashed, and unkempt young men were unlikely to impress drivers whilst those who presented themselves decently, looked at the vehicle from whom they were begging a lift and smiled, were in with a chance.

It worked and some seven weeks later he reappeared looking fit, remarkably clean and tidy and a lot wiser. His route had taken him across Italy and into Yugoslavia then down into Bosnia. Here he had met up with both Serbs and Croats, living rough with them in the hills. He reached Sarajevo and from time to time heard gunfire and saw much evidence of the bitter struggle. The sights he saw, the people he met and the tales that were told had left a deep and lasting impression on the young eighteen-year-old who had seen and heard at first hand just how terrible such conflicts can be.

He had enjoyed his rugby at school in England and was delighted to find that Lavaur, like virtually every centre of population in south-west France, had its own thriving rugby club. He joined almost immediately and continued to play until he returned to England. Many of our visitors have asked us about the rugby in France – how it started, why they are so keen on the game and how it is that the French often do so well? There are a number of possible answers most associated with three principal points – the character of the individual, the attitude of the family and community, and the long, very well-organised season.

We have found the Frenchman of the south-west are not far removed from the Cornishman or Welshman in character. Most who play rugby are physically tough and competitive to the point of being combative. There is always an intensely strong team spirit, sometimes bordering on the frenzied. They take enormous pride in the club and go onto the pitch worked up close to bursting point, determined to destroy the opposition. Individually they love to show off their skills, run with the ball and tend to be a bit prima donna-ish, their spirits rising or falling with the fortunes of the game.

Here in France there is only one centre of sport in each town and that is the local *Stade*. Anybody who wants to play goes there and joins the town club be he a youth at the *lycée*, a young soldier from the barracks, a kid from the junior school or whoever. The efforts and fortunes of the town are therefore concentrated unlike in England. When Jamie, my younger son, was playing for the Winchester Colts there was the town club, a Sixth Form College club, the local military team and another school club. The French would not understand this diversification of resources or dispersion of talent and, looked at from here, they have a good point.

All support is centralised and there is just the one focal point for everything including financial support. As a result the facilities are superb, the coaching and administration coordinated and local support focused. Lavaur boasts two floodlit rugby pitches. The principal one has a grandstand holding upwards of 750 spectators, the pitch is surrounded by the all-weather athletics track, there are car parking facilities and sometimes there is pre-match entertainment.

When there is a local derby more than 750 spectators will each pay 50 Francs or more at the turnstiles. The junior pitch, where Tristan played, has its own floodlights, car park, excellent training facilities and clubhouse. When Tristan played away from home the team would go off by coach, be fed on the way and we never received a bill.

Nowhere in the UK would such facilities be found in a small provincial town. Winchester, many times the size of Lavaur, had nothing to compare with all this and South Molton (my home town in Devon, not a lot smaller than Lavaur) has little more than a reasonably flat field on the outskirts of the town, rudimentary and spartan facilities by comparison and can only dream of floodlights.

The whole of French rugby is coordinated into a multitude of Leagues that are contested throughout the long season which lasts two months longer than in England. The Lavaur 1st XV has its league as do the 2nd XV, the Juniors, the Cadets, the Minimes and even the younger teams. The whole town takes a close interest in the progress of all the teams with results and league tables being posted in a cafe in Centre Ville. Lavaur had better do well or the town would want to know why.

And then finally there is the actual support for the teams as they run out in the town colours. When Jamie was playing for Winchester Colts they fielded an outstanding team with one boy going on to gain a number of caps for Scotland, another playing for England Colts and several more for Hampshire Colts. The fixture list was impressive with clubs such as Bath and Harlequins being regular opponents. I used to take him down to play and then stay on to support. Sometimes there were as many as ten of us on the touchline – and one of them was Patch.

On away fixtures the boys would squeeze into a few cars and that was that. When Tristan ran out for the Lavaur Cadets he ran through a tunnel of cheering spectators on to the pitch lined with 3-400 supporters. Family, friends, other teams and many from the town would be there, week in week out, in all weathers.

Once the game had started I noticed two other important points, one concerning the refereeing. The game in England at youth and junior level is dominated by the whistle. Over-zealous referees blow up for every tiny infringement and time and again the game is killed stone dead, the youngsters getting more and more frustrated and dispirited at not being allowed to get going.

Here in France I am quite certain that the referees take a more lenient attitude to minor infringements with a result that the game flows. The boys are encouraged to run, run and run again, passing the ball up and down the line, the backs and forwards supporting each other. Minor infringements are often overlooked, the game is kept alive and it is a joy to participate. Occasionally, of course, it all backfires and the players take the law into their own hands when all hell breaks loose, much to the delight of the crowd.

Finally the French play the squad system far better than the English who, at least until the professional game appeared, tended to play just the best XV, replacements coming on only when an injury occurred. The result was that the other lads who had come along for a game rarely got onto the field and soon became disenchanted with being for ever on the touchline. Here the coaches let as many members of the squad as possible have a run, perhaps for no more than twenty minutes or so but at least they get onto the field and feel part of the show.

Put all this together and therein, I believe, lies the recipe for the modern French game. When the going is bad, one is witness to the volatile side of their nature – petulance, bad temper and sulking, the team often arguing amongst themselves and sometimes falling apart. All of this I am prepared to accept for, when it comes together, the French, at any level, are a joy to watch.

Take the French XV on a warm spring afternoon, give them a firm pitch and a dry ball and watch them cut loose. Few can match them on these occasions and they are universally acclaimed as one of the most exciting teams in the world. I would suggest this national flair stems from countless grounds around south-west France where youngsters who are desperate to succeed and impress are supported so strongly by the family, by the community and indeed by the State itself.

I have been told that there is a soccer ground somewhere in Toulouse rather as there is in Auckland or Cape Town but the taxi driver will give you a pretty strange look in his mirror and query your instructions if you ask to be taken there rather than the Stade Rugby.

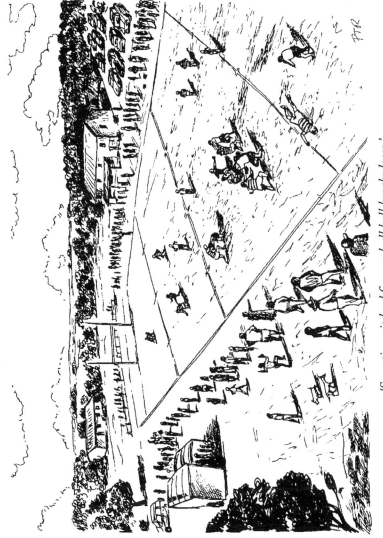

'Sometimes it backfires and all hell breaks loose.'

109

# CHAPTER IX

# Life Around Us

*Dogs and cats. Alice. Le Muret – our ruins.*
*The Romans. Gaillac wine.*

One of the first things we noticed on arrival at Bosc Lebat was that, just as in any large country house with numerous outbuildings, the rodent population made determined efforts to join us once the weather turned cold. Patch had been having a marvellous time from day one, rushing hither and thither, marking his quarry under huge piles of timber or behind pieces of equipment in the barns.

However, the threat of an invasion such as this called for action and a major operation began by removing any sources of food from the animals, setting numerous traps and laying poison near any of the runs we had spotted. The house had been empty for some time before we moved in so the creatures had quite rightly assumed ownership of the place. Much to their discomfort we challenged them for possession. We wanted our house back and called for reinforcements in the shape of two young cats.

When I lived in Winchester, Patch was given the task of keeping the garden clear of cats. He applied himself to this vigorously and, when he found two cats had dared to install themselves at Bosc Lebat, he could not believe his luck and decided to sort things out. We had to play this very carefully and for a couple of weeks there was an armed truce as both parties studied each other with deep suspicion.

Then, during supper one evening, war broke out. From the dining room came the sound of battle and amidst fearful shrieks and barks the two young cats flew into the kitchen, one leaping straight onto Rachel's back and from there to the top of the fridge. The second hit the kitchen worktop at speed sliding along the surface scattering plates, glasses and food in all directions.

After a moment's silence Patch skidded to a halt at the door unsure whether to be pleased with himself or to look suitably contrite. He chose the latter course thus avoiding our wrath but we knew the performance would be repeated. The poor old chap was lonely down there and needed company so we set about finding him a companion.

We had already been to see the vet to make sure that Patch and now the cats had all the right jabs for this part of the world. Jean-Michel Bonifacy, a delightful man who loved animals and always made a great fuss of whoever was brought to see him, told us that from time to time a stray would be passed to him. We asked him to let us know when the next one was brought in and we would come over and make a decision about it.

Nearly six months passed and we had all but forgotten our request. Patch had somehow forced himself to accept the presence of the cats. He attempted just one further head-on confrontation resulting in a sharp swipe across the nose and a loud yelp from the dog. Thereafter they all kept their distance although on one occasion trouble flared up when Patch, now conducting flanking operations rather than frontal assaults, laid in ambush by the cat flap, knobbling his enemies as they came through. I could not but give full marks to the cunning old dog! However as far as the rodents were concerned Patch and the cats formed a strong team and between them had given the creatures an unpleasant introduction to the British occupation.

One day the phone rang, it was Jean-Michel to say that a little stray had been handed in to him and asked if we were interested. Rachel had, up to now, been very much a cat person, treating all dogs with disdain or suspicion – she and Patch had just about established a working relationship before eventually becoming good friends.

She announced loftily that she, accompanied by Tristan, would go and examine the creature and that she alone would make the decision. She did not want any old dog in her house. When she told me that it was a three-month-old bitch puppy I assured her that she would be back with it. And sure enough she was – Alice had arrived. Half Yorkie half Tibetan terrier, she was a minute scrap of life and we wondered how anyone could have let something like that wander out of their lives. Patch was immediately on guard – two cats were bad enough but now a new female around the place meant his position was to be further threatened.

I was uneasy about it also because the little dog had a full tummy, was not in the least bit afraid of us and was almost house trained. I was worried that we might get a call from Jean-Michel to say that there had been a dreadful mistake and that the owner had come to him. I decided that we would give it one week after which Alice would have identified with us and there would be no going back. We kept our fingers crossed and on the seventh morning I announced that it was now too late, Alice was here to stay.

Patch took his time and one afternoon decided to assert his authority. We were sitting in the garden when suddenly he jumped on Alice, spun her over and gave her a full-blooded session of Jack Russell bared teeth and savage snarls. The poor little mite was terrified and as soon as I pulled him off, Alice leapt into Rachel's arms squealing with fright. But Patch had never closed his jaws even slightly on her – had he so wished he could have killed her in a trice as if she was a young rabbit. He was just letting everyone know who was boss around the place. Alice did not contest the issue there and then but bided her time.

The dust settled and a few days later we were having lunch under the chestnuts. Alice was curled up at Rachel's feet keeping a wary eye out for the monster, when he appeared at the front door with his ball in his mouth. He walked to within a few feet of the table, put the ball down and, tail wagging, nosed it towards Alice. She looked up, moved to go forward, stopped to look back at us, checking that this was for real and then ran up to Patch, rolling onto her back, mustering all the affection she could.

Patch stood there watching and Alice, her composure now recovered, started playing with the ball whilst darting to and fro from the sanctuary of Rachel's feet whenever she thought this chap was getting too close for comfort. From that moment they have been inseparable. Patch adores his little companion whilst she, like every good woman, has got her man firmly under control.

Two dogs and two cats, Bosc Lebat seemed crowded but no guests just yet. The land beyond the orchard and our southern boundary rises gently upwards to a crest line where there is an old ruined farmhouse. It belonged to our neighbour – Jacques Gaudebert – who ran his flock of sheep through the land as soon as there was a swathe of grass. Jacques, a bachelor, lived in the farm beyond our big wood with his mother, a delightful old lady who looked after her son and, in spite of being over eighty, kept the house and garden as well.

I often saw Jacques around his farm and, since he had rented our two fields for the princely sum of two fat lambs a year, he was often around Bosc Lebat. His story was that his parents had lived in Morocco where he and his nine brothers and sisters were born. When the troubles in North Africa degenerated into a bloody uprising and French settlers were being killed, de Gaulle brought out all those he could and relocated them in the rural areas of France. They became known as *Pieds Noirs* and in the early stages were treated with a certain amount of reserve by the indigenous French on account of the generous grants and loans they were given to help them set up their new way of life.

Most turned to agriculture and a number of families settled here. The old ruins, known as Le Muret, were deserted at about this time when many French families left the countryside to try their luck in the cities and larger towns. Jacques took on the land but, in order to avoid paying taxes on the property, took off the roof and let the old farm fall into disrepair. There it was on the crest just beyond our land looking down at Bosc Lebat and we were glad that nobody lived there.

It is an evocative spot with a marvellous view across to Lavaur. Behind it at the top of the short track up to the road the Black Mountains can be seen on the eastern horizon as can a jagged row of Pyrennean peaks in the far distance. Part of our deal with Jacques was that we and our guests could walk up there to enjoy the wonderful views. Jacques had long since got used to the dogs who loved the place as it abounds with rabbits and hares.

Furthermore, the land around the old farmstead had never been treated with any form of chemicals, weed killers or fertilizers. The result was a wonderful proliferation of wild flowers and, come summer, the air would be thick with a multitude of brightly coloured butterflies – the spot had become a tiny wildlife sanctuary.

Occasionally Jacques would call in when passing the house and the next time he did so we had just finished the swimming pool. We were rather pleased with the progress but by now we had all but run out of funds and there was still much to be done. However we could count ourselves lucky that the pool was in and set in a secluded and south-facing position.

We were about to have lunch when the dogs told us we had visitors. It was Jacques who had brought a well-known *immobilier* from Lavaur with him. They asked us if they could have a few words. Chairs were pulled up, a bottle of wine and glasses produced and we were told that Jacques, being short of cash, had decided to put the ruins on the market along with a few acres around them. It was a good position, the *immobilier* interjected quite unnecessarily for our benefit. There was mains water up there, a good access track to the road and, as it had been a dwelling, it would be sure to get planning permission. Were we interested?

The thunderbolt had struck fair and square. A house up there would totally dominate our gardens and the pool in particular. Imagine teenage music, motorbikes, the smell of cooking, barking dogs. We talked about it for a while and they left knowing full well our reaction. After a hurried lunch we went up to have a look at Le Muret. There was no doubt that the place would be snapped up. We just had to buy it but for how much and where was that sort of money coming from? We rang the *notaire* who had dealt with the sale of Bosc Lebat, the one who had come over here as a boy and played with the children.

Jacques Renaud knew the ruins and agreed to come over and discuss the matter with us. Together we walked slowly around the old farmstead and from time to time he would stop and reminisce about the past. He loved the spot and said that we should go for it, although Jacques' price was on the high side, stressing that it would add more to the value of our estate than we would have to pay. However, he added, if we did not buy it and a house was put there then the value of our property would surely fall steeply. That was it. Cold logic like that in amongst all the nostalgic memories sent us to the bank.

The manager came out to see us. She was a delightful lady, warm, very friendly and we enjoyed talking to her. However Patch who, for some reason had taken an aversion to the French, gave her a good blood-letting nip just as we were getting down to business. For a moment I thought our banker was going to slam down the grill and march out in high dudgeon, but Anne Marie was a star – a professional banker too – and we drew up a plan to buy Le Muret. Today it is ours, the sheep still graze the pasture and our guests still take a delight in wandering up to savour the peace and admire the views.

Beyond Le Muret there is another slightly higher ridge along the top of which runs a well-used bridle path known as La Voie Romaine. The original track runs from St Sulpice where the River Agout, having passed through Lavaur, joins with the larger River Tarn. St Sulpice is some twelve miles west of us and the narrow, ancient road runs on past us in a south-easterly direction towards Carcassonne and then on to the sea.

There is an excellent small Roman museum in Albi, next door to the cathedral in the old Bishops' Palace, and in here they have a map of the

Roman occupation in the Tarn on which La Voie Romaine is clearly marked. It was not a major route but, more likely, a minor administrative road built to help the Roman officials get about their business. The whole community would have used the road, perhaps paying a toll for the privilege.

One of the wells on our land is known as the Roman Well and lies just a couple of hundred yards from the road. Wells were the centre of village life in those days and it is easy to imagine Roman soldiers or servants of wealthy travellers being sent down from the road to refill the gourds and goat skins before going on their way.

The well would have been a centre for gossip and the passage of information as the travellers passed on their stories to the villagers who in turn would impart local news. Fruit and vegetables would have been sold by the side of the well and perhaps village maidens would flirt with the young Roman soldiers as they waited their turn by the water. The Romans of that period were great farmers, builders and engineers as well as colonists.

The secret of their success was not in open conflict with the local people but fraternisation and inter-marriage. Almost 80 per cent of the Roman Army in Gaul were auxiliaries or mercenaries, many recruited locally from the tribes of the area. However, everybody was answerable to Rome, and when there was trouble with the local tribes, it would have been suppressed ruthlessly, the miscreants being cruelly executed, their bodies left hanging, as at Golgotha, a grim warning for the remainder to pay heed to the law of Rome.

The ruins of Le Muret are above the well on a small knoll that is in a commanding position at the head of the valley. Here, in the old gardens there is another well amongst the wild figs and the layout of a Roman Villa. The site is in a significant position being so close to the road and it is possible that this may have been the residence of some minor official charged with the administration of the area. A few years ago I asked what the chances were of an archeological dig taking place. Sadly, archaeology is always a low priority for funds and I was told that, although Le Muret was on the list there were many other sites awaiting their turn.

The field beyond the old villa has a piece of rough unbroken ground in the centre. It is the site of some old catacombs, left untouched by the farmers, where an archeological dig took place some years previously. The finds that were unearthed are now in the local museum and are ample proof that a sizeable community inhabited the land around Bosc Lebat all those centuries ago. Perhaps one day we will be able to explore the sites further.

While there are a few vineyards around Lavaur, the town of Gaillac on the Tarn is well known for its wines. The mixture of soil, shale and gently sloping hillsides are excellent for the vine and it is often claimed that the Romans developed the first vineyards in France along the banks of the Tarn. This is difficult to accept and it is now widely believed that wine production was common throughout this area many centuries before the Roman Empire existed.

The claim about Gaillac is an attractive thought but I, too, have my reservations. The Romans are believed to have first arrived in Gaul around 100 BC – some forty years before Caesar took it upon himself to subdue the tribes. It is widely acknowledged that the Romans first landed on the coast at Narbonne or at least developed Narbonne as the port which linked the first expedition with Rome. I have often tried to put myself in the position of that first commander and looked at the problems he would have faced.

As soon as they had landed the troops would have been given the task of securing the immediate area. They would have pushed inland for some distance, securing the high ground, then constructed a network of defences. Within these the expedition would have made first a base then a harbour to provide the vital link with Rome.

Orders would have gone out to the administrators to set up some form of food production so that those committed permanently to life around Narbonne could sustain themselves, rather than having to forage further and further afield. It would not have taken the farmers and *vignerons* long to have realised the full potential of the soil in the area and, as wine was part of the staple diet, vines would have been planted here at the earliest opportunity and for certain several years before the Romans had pushed inland as far as Gaillac.

Once firmly ashore the commander would have probed inland cautiously, sending out scouting parties to see what lay ahead and to make contact with the local inhabitants. The men would have moved slowly in full combat order, their heavy equipment moving behind in baggage trains under guard. The countryside would have been unbroken and, even in the relatively flat coastal areas, progress would have been difficult – perhaps no more than a few kilometres at a time.

At the end of each day's march they would have halted and consolidated their position, establishing a well-fortified forward base, opening up and securing their lines of communication behind them. The Roman Army was basically infantry and the legions would have built fortifications wherever they stopped, sometimes even if only for the night. Such an effort would have slowed down their overall progress even further.

All the while reconnaissance patrols would have been probing further ahead, selecting the best routes and taking no chances with the local tribes. It would have been a long, difficult and slow operation with many setbacks. Several months would have passed between leaving the sanctuary of Narbonne and setting up a firm base at Gaillac on the Tarn – far removed from jumping into the car and dashing up the Narbonne/Toulouse/Albi motorways of today.

It is thus fair to assume that the Romans would have established extensive vineyards along the coast for their own consumption long before creating others further inland. The hillsides around Narbonne – where now the wines of Corbieres and Minervois are grown – can, with every justification, claim to have been the first Roman vineyards in France.

There is no doubt, however, that Gaillac became an important centre for Roman activities in this part of France at some later date. Once the expedition into the interior had reached this point, once the military situation had been brought under control and once the community had established itself, then the vines would have been planted. However, Gaillac's claim might not be entirely misleading for the area could well have been the first site for wines as a commercial venture in the interior, developed by the Romans as they pushed ever deeper into Gaul.

What is beyond doubt is that, once established, the wines of Gaillac became famous and much sought after, far superior in quality to the early wines from Bordeaux and other areas. Many Frenchmen challenge this point, believing that the great vineyards of today have always been so, but when I refer them to their own histories of French wine, I am given a Gallic shrug, a rueful grin and they have to agree.

Having chosen to live here I am delighted to say that one reason for the rise in popularity of early Gaillac wine was due to the great demand from England. In fact so great was the superiority of the Gaillac wines that the wine growers in Bordeaux levied a tax on each barrel that came through the port in a brazen attempt to live off the competition even if they could not compete with it. Later the Gaillac wines were even used to blend with the inferior Bordeaux in an attempt to improve the quality of the local stock.

More recently, of course, the great vineyards of Bordeaux and the Medoc have become renowned the world over, but there are those who believe that Gaillac wines could yet regain their former reputation and even now they are beginning to force their way back into wider recognition. The better wines of Gaillac are a delight to drink and we take pride in serving them to our guests, many of whom claim to have a discerning taste for a good wine. They are rarely disappointed.

The Romans certainly made their presence felt in this corner of France and much evidence of their occupation remains to this day. Amongst it all is our Voie Romaine along which we and our guests love to walk and admire the superb scenery in every direction. Throughout the length of the walk the Pyrenees can be seen clearly far away on the southern horizon when the haze permits, whilst to the east the ridge line of the Black Mountains rises to over 3,000'. Finally, the whole vista of the Tarn rolls away to the north where occasionally it is possible to make out the blue smudge of the Aveyron hills in the far distance.

# CHAPTER X

## *People and Places*

*Annie of La Voie Romaine. Our valley. Massac hamlet.*
*Chateau Seran – the lady of the Irises. My bad friend Jerry.*
*Time is running out and the guests are coming.*

Of all the many walks around Bosc Lebat the one we like best is
along the Voie Romaine. Not only are the distant views superb but
I love to go up there and gaze down into the head of the valley. There,
beyond Le Muret, I can see the outline of Bosc Lebat all but hidden
behind the trees. The day after we had become the proud owners of Le
Muret I took a walk along La Voie Romaine with the dogs and had
come to a point where I could see Le Muret in the middle distance. I
slowed to admire the view when just in front of me and half hidden in
the long grass I saw something.

It was a body lying face down, head resting on hands, legs slightly
apart. There was no sign of life but perhaps the person was asleep. There
was a difference though – the body, save for a pair of minute black
knickers around one ankle, was stark naked. This, I thought with some
concern, might get a bit tricky. If the body was a dead one then it was
obviously a pretty juicy murder and I did not fancy the idea of getting
caught up in all that. However, if it was alive then who, why and what?

I moved closer and the body stirred, sat up and turned towards me. It
was, without any doubt very much a live one, extremely feminine, in the
fullness of life and very attractive at that. She was also quite unabashed
by my presence.

Stretching lazily, she ran her hands through her long hair and said sleepily, 'Oh, I am sorry. I must have fallen asleep.' And with that she stood up. 'I was looking down at those ruins. What a lovely spot, I would like to meet the owner as I am looking for something like that.'

Without a flicker of self-consciousness she casually brushed the grass from her body before bending over to pick up a skimpy little white top which she pulled slowly over her head. I looked around somewhat apprehensively. What if Jacques Gaudebert or Odd Job or the Bells should appear now? A fine old tale about Monsieur Le Colonel this would make at the Saturday Market.

Still clad in just her outrageously immodest T-shirt that concealed nothing of any consequence, she looked around for her pair of white shorts. Wriggling herself into them she pulled up the zip with a giggle and a resounding 'Voila!'

Not sure if I really had seen what I thought I had, we got talking and I found that Annie was down from Paris and staying nearby. She loved walking the countryside and, as I was now only too aware, sunbathing. She returned to the subject of the ruins and I had to tell her that we were now the owners. Still fascinated she asked if she could go and explore. I told her that I was on my way home and I would gladly show her the way.

We reached Le Muret and she was enchanted. Walking down past the ruins we came to a glade where some huge oaks provided shade from the sun. It was a sheltered spot, a place of ancient habitation as the tumuli amongst the trees indicated. There were some piles of stones half covered with grass and, further still, some very old fruit trees – a sure sign of previous dwellings.

As she looked around her I could see that Annie was enthralled with the place. 'Are they really yours?' she asked.

'Yes,' I replied her, 'we bought them just yesterday.'

'Will you allow me to come and hide away here?'

'Of course,' I nodded. 'You are more than welcome.'

'You are very kind,' she replied 'I think I will stay a while now. Will

'Stretching lazily she ran her hands through her long hair.'

you stay with me?' And with that she slipped out of her clothes and settled back in the sun.

'I think perhaps it would be better if I went on my way,' I told her, trying to ignore the devil that had appeared on my shoulder. I got back and recounted the tale to Rachel. She looked at me sharply, unable to decide whether I had been dreaming or had indeed had such an encounter. 'You had better ask the dogs,' I said giving her a squeeze.

Another of our favourite walks from the house is around the valley. Every day one of us takes the dogs down the road towards Massac and back up the track. It is just about two miles and the idea is to take the edge off their energy or they will slink off to the woods and spend half the day rabbiting, returning covered in mud, ticks, fleas and anything else that lurks down the burrows.

There is an old badger set in the wood too and when we are returning home at night, we sometimes see them in the car headlights as they move around hunting for their supper. Foxes are here also and, on a still evening in mid-winter, we can often hear the vixens calling in search of a mate. Between them all they keep the rabbits more or less under control but each winter we get a team in with nets and ferrets to keep numbers down.

Very occasionally we come across the small deer – *chevreuil.* They are very timid and stay close to the cover of the larger woods but sometimes we see them feeding. Last year I watched a couple less than a kilometre from the house and I was sure that, somewhere nearby, they had tucked their fawns away in the dense cover.

Bosc Lebat used to own nearly all the land in the valley but, as the family had explained, the previous owner sold much of it. His profession, that of agricultural adviser, took him away from the farm as he went about his business. The money he made from the land went into bringing the house and buildings into the twentieth century. We have records of the community here almost as far back as the Revolution. In those days between fifteen and twenty people lived at

Bosc Lebat with many more close by. Apart from the main family there was the farrier, the carter, the guardian and cowman as well as local labour that would come in to work on a daily basis as this was the principal farm in the area.

Almost every day and certainly on market days somebody would have taken a pony and trap or cart into Lavaur to fetch whatever produce they could not grow on the estate. Most of the food would have been grown in the gardens and orchards around the house and the community here must have been fully occupied, everyone having their own place and their own jobs to do.

On special occasions, such as harvesting, extra labour would have come in from Massac or one of the small hamlets nearby such as St Germier or Pratviel. Everyone would have chatted away in Occitane rather than in French as we know it today. When there were weddings or christenings or when harvest time came round there must have been great parties in the orchards or barns to celebrate the events. The name Bosc Lebat is the Occitane for *Bois Levée* or High Wood as the house stands under the wood at the head of the valley.

Massac, just over a mile from us, is a small community centred in part around the church and convent at the top of the hill alongside the Mairie. Very soon after we arrived Rachel and I went along to the Maire and introduced ourselves. Sometime earlier we had been warned by a rather dubious British expatriot to be on our guard.

'You want to be careful,' he urged. 'France is a dodgy place and full of informers. Everything you do is noted down and records are kept.'

I stared at the fellow in disbelief. 'What the hell do you think we are going to get up to, running drugs or something?'

'Well, just look out, they'll put everything down on paper. That's all the advice I can give.'

We knocked on the door of the tiny Mairie and were met warmly by the Maire's secretary. Madame Marty could not have done more for us and, in those difficult early days, helped us patiently with the numerous baffling forms and papers we had to sign. Her husband is mayor of the next-door hamlet and farms some of the land in our valley. Our small field in front of Bosc Lebat was badly overgrown when we arrived and I asked Madame Marty if she knew of a local contractor who could do the job for us.

A week or so later her husband appeared with tractor and plough, did the job for us and steadfastly refused any payment for his troubles, waving me away with a broad smile. We see our own mayor often, especially after bad weather or heavy rain, when he tours the area to see if we have had any trouble. The mayors here in France have much more authority than their counterparts in the UK who are little more than community figureheads. Monsieur Rainier has often picked up the phone on our behalf when we have been stuck for help and we are delighted that he and his secretary do know about us.

Gathered around the Mairie, just down the hill, are two or three substantial farms and around each one of these are clustered small groups of cottages. When our roses arrived from England I hitched the trailer to the car and called on one of the farms where I knew there were some cows and a great heap of old manure outside the cowshed. As politely as I could and in my best French I asked if I could fill my trailer. The family gathered at the door to see this stranger who smiled politely at them but spoke gibberish.

Unfortunately, I had got myself into a dreadful muddle and asked instead if I could possibly have a trailer load of spare household rubbish. The family, young, old and very old, stood together in the doorway staring silently at this foreigner from the other end of the valley, their eyes wide and mouths open, uncomprehending. I tried again but got no further and was about to try my luck as a refuse collector elsewhere when the farmer arrived.

Gently he coaxed the truth from me such as a psychiatrist might talk to a seriously mad patient, then suddenly burst into guffaws of laughter, slapping me on the back. His family saw the funny side of it all as well and seemed mightily relieved that their new neighbour had not gone completely off his rocker. I was hustled into the big farm kitchen whereupon a large bottle of powerful Eau de Vie was produced and toasts were drunk to the manure, household rubbish and everything else before I was sent off up the road, my trailer loaded up with good rich cow dung for my roses.

One or two new houses have been put up since our arrival but Massac remains today much as it has been for generations – a small, homely hamlet, inhabited by a tight-knit and friendly community. Most of those of working age these days go off by bus or car to Lavaur or Toulouse but in times gone by nearly everyone would have had a job on one of the farms, in the woods or would have been employed by the Mairie working on the roads.

There is another small hamlet near Massac called Seran and sometimes the two are linked together, known collectively as Massac-Seran. In Seran there is what was once a proud chateau. Chateau Seran is now rather a sad place, a shadow of its former self, but has nonetheless quite a history to it. Soon after we arrived the son of one of the Chateau's previous owners came and called on us.

Over a cup of tea he told a tale of an earlier lady of the Chateau who was obviously a character of some spirit in that she had a habit of bestowing her favours on numerous members of the local gentry. After each tryst she would award her lover flowers or a plant to commemorate the occasion. Legend has it that those whose attentions impressed her most were awarded irises and that the colour of the iris flower bore witness to how highly she rated the performance of her beau.

It was sometime in early spring when the visitor called and when we had finished our tea I took him out and showed him around the gardens. The irises were at their absolute peak – a magnificent display of every colour imaginable from white and the palest of yellows right through the spectrum to the deepest of purples. 'What do you make of that little lot?' I enquired.

'Well,' he replied after some thought, 'she was quite a lady, you know, and there were some big, strong lads up here.'

When we first arrived the Chateau was occupied by an Englishman and his family. I liked Jerry Baker and his wife Rosemary. I liked him because he was nothing less than a loveable old rogue who was up to all sorts of mischief. Some British people we met advised us not to go near the dreadful man, his wife or the Chateau. That made me even more determined to get to know them although I swore I would never enter into a business agreement with Jerry.

He was trying to renovate the place and convert a number of the outbuildings into cottages and sell them on. Rumour had it that after finishing the first project one of his party sold the place time and again, eventually slipping away before the numerous different owners arrived, each one claiming ownership.

He advertised for cheap labour quite brazenly in the UK press, offering a wonderful holiday, all the food and drink one could want plus £50 per week in return for a good honest day's work. Rogues, philanderers and day-dreamers were attracted by Jerry's advertising like moths to a lamp. He had them all there and worked them hard.

They played mighty hard too and on more than one occasion their antics were brought to the attention of the local gendarmes. The only problem for us was that the good folk of Lavaur would sometimes get us mixed up, thinking it was us who lived at Chateau Seran rather than Jerry and his hellraisers. I thoroughly enjoyed Jerry's company but wasted no time in putting this one right.

Rosemary kept a number of horses there and from time to time they would come riding past with some of their guests and would stop for a chat. Sometimes I used to go over there and stare in amazement at what they had taken on and how they were setting about it. When I thought how small our operation was in comparison, yet how expensive it all was in spite of our ruthless budgeting, I doubted that they would ever see the thing through.

Once every six weeks or so Jerry and I would go off for a long, slow lunch and he used to keep me amused with the tales of life at the Chateau. There always seemed to be a large number of youngsters on the site. Heaven knows how they all lived there together or where they all slept but, if what Jerry told me was anything like the truth, then there were high jinks indeed.

Of course it could not last and in the end Jerry did a mysterious deal with a local *immobilier* and one night they slipped away under cover of darkness. Country life is the same the world over and if one lives out there the characters come and go. The tittle tattle and gossip filters down the grapevine and, fuelled by the Saturday markets and village fêtes, gets better and better as it does the rounds. Jerry was a character, good for a laugh and I missed the old cove.

But I must put such thoughts aside and get back to Bosc Lebat where, in the last few weeks before the guests arrived, life was speeding up. In spite of our occasional sorties we were tied to the place in a desperate rush to get everything ready as we had advertised and to give the old house as much of a polish as time would permit. Before we left England we had received a number of offers of help. Whilst well intended, come the hour, most of those who offered their services could not get away. We thought that this would be the case and had not banked on any reinforcements, but we were lucky and, just when we needed help, we got a couple of phone calls.

When I had come out to have a look around a few years previously I had come with an old friend – Tony Gauvain. One evening he called and asked if we could do with an extra pair of hands. It was an unbelievably kind offer, there were no strings attached, no hidden agenda such as calling in on the way through: just a simple offer of help. Many years ago we had been together at Sandhurst and later at the Army Staff College. Some time after that he too had commanded his regiment in Northern Ireland.

It was great to see him again and catch up on his news. True to his word he had brought just old gardening clothes together with lots of elbow grease. For a week he scraped, painted, washed and polished allowing us to get on with a number of other jobs. An old girlfriend of

Rachel's came out a week later and she too turned her hand to anything we asked of her. Karen and Tony gave our efforts a tremendous boost at just the right time.

The third pair of hands came in the shape of the son of an old friend of mine. Alan Ladd and I had grown up together on Exmoor and we had served together during my last command at Netheravon. His younger son, George, wanted to take a break from his office routine and offered himself to us for nearly three weeks. We were, at that time, starting to landscape the area around the pool and George's visit coincided with the stirling efforts of Monsieur Ricard of swimming pool fame.

We had decided to put a rose pergola at the bottom of the steps leading to the pool and this involved a good deal of back-breaking work with the oak beams and concrete foundations. George worked like a Trojan and it is difficult to see how we would have got ourselves ready without the efforts of these three heroes. We had been warned that there were helpers and there were helpers. We should be wary of those who might be after a short break in the sun or the key to the cellar, but these three did us proud.

Although the end of June had been our target date, we had been asked by a couple if they could come a month earlier. We warned them that it would not be the haven of peace and quiet they might have been expecting but they were determined and so it was to be the end of May that our doors would be opened to the public. We had had little time to realise it but the locals told us we had just come through one of the wettest winters and springs on record, but now the skies cleared and we saw Bosc Lebat in all its spring glory. The *gîte* was not to be occupied for a number of weeks so we shifted our attention there while around the *manoir* there descended an aura of calm, albeit a temporary one.

We had been in France for seven months by now but in that time had managed to settle ourselves, had reshaped and renovated the house so that we could take guests, had put in the pool and had all but refitted the *gîte*. It had been something of a race although I had a sneaking feeling that, had it not been imperative for us to get it all up and running, we would have been fiddling around with this and that for ever and a day.

It was now time to change tack completely and all of a sudden we realised that we had no idea of how to handle paying guests in the house. Ordinary guests or friends are simple enough. You know who is coming and subconsciously you switch on to the particular characters concerned. Everybody needs to be treated differently and you would hardly treat an elderly maiden aunt in the same way as you would an old chum from the far-off days of riotous youth.

However, with friends and acquaintances you did at least know in advance who and what to expect. Hotel guests were, so we imagined, fairly straightforward in that everybody knew what was what, who could go where, and where the barriers were. It was a relatively simple business to face the guests under these circumstances.

But those whom we were about to receive were a bit of both – they were total strangers about whom we knew absolutely nothing yet they were coming into our house as house guests, using our linen and bathrooms, eating off our china, drinking our wine and sitting with us in the garden or lazing by the pool.

How on earth were we meant to behave and whatever were we going do if a particular visit went horribly wrong? I shuddered at the thought of having to take Archie Shaw's stentorian advice. And what were they going to expect? How would they wish to be treated by us – the owners cum servants? A few weeks before, thoughts like this had conjured up all sorts of amusing possibilities, but now time had run on and it was not quite so funny any more.

We sat and pondered this for a while then just threw our hands into the air and shouted with laughter. We decided to forget any sort of formalities whatsoever and treat them all as our friends. We would just carry on as normal, business as usual – Mr and Mrs K-F at home – and if they did not like it, to hell with it!

# CHAPTER XI

## *Guests – and Others*

*Early guests and some of their moments that tested the system!*

The morning of 27 May broke in much the same way as any other, but for us it was a red letter day: that afternoon our first guests were due to arrive. Now, after all the planning and preparation, it was to be the moment of truth. We were both somewhat apprehensive about it as we still had so much to do on the house. They had asked if they might come early and, as this was to be the case, we had told them they would have to take us as they found us. They seemed perfectly happy with this idea so, to some small extent, we were off the hook.

The great spring dawn chorus serenaded the arrival of the big day at Bosc Lebat. Dawn broke slowly in the eastern sky behind the big wood, gradually the sun rose, filtering its way through the treetops and along the southern skyline. I was up soon after first light and decided to take the dogs out earlier than usual. I went up the long slope past the ruins to the ancient road where I sat quietly and took in the magnificent vista of the Tarn waking to a late spring morning.

Some of the valleys below were filled with an early mist, all were in deep shadow but up on the hilltops the sun was already warm on the face. Far away on the southern horizon the mountains were bathed in sunlight, the snow on the high peaks a magnificent rose pink in the morning light. It was a good time to sit and think about the day ahead – or about anything else for that matter – the world seemed to be a quiet and peaceful place at this early hour.

I walked past Jacques' farm and saw that he too was up, already, tending the ewes and lambs that had been gathered into one of his big barns for the night. On again, around the head of the valley before dropping down to Bosc Lebat for breakfast. At this time we were in the middle of preparing the dining-room walls for papering. It was a fiddly, messy job that necessitated hours up the ladder working away at imperfections in the surfaces. I loathed the very idea of it all.

Halfway through the morning I had had enough and went down to clean the pool. Swimming pools do not stay clean on their own and keeping a large one in a condition acceptable to guests takes about an hour and a half each day by the time one has cleaned the pool house, all the furniture and the terraces, as well as the pool itself.

We were beginning to find that our morning chores in and around the house took up a fair amount of time but from now on we would have the extra dimension of guests wandering downstairs wanting to get on with their breakfast. They were going to be our number one priority so we would have to reorganise the early part of our day to fit in around them or there would be a muddle and everyone would start getting excited.

At about five in the afternoon Bill and Doreen Foster came slowly up the drive and our show was on the road. They were a delightful couple who introduced themselves by apologising profusely for imposing themselves on us several weeks early. Bill had been to my old school, Sherborne, some time before me and had spotted the article I had been asked to write for the Old Shirburnian magazine.

He had had an interesting life as a journalist spending a number of years in Washington for *The Times*. Doreen was a great gardener and from the first day we spent hours discussing how I might improve the gardens while, at the same time, decreasing the workload – every gardener's dream. They were great fun and in the evenings we would sit in the garden contemplating how things might work out with our new venture and between us we dreamed up some wonderful scenarios.

*'Jacques was up, tending his ewes and lambs.'*

Bill assured as that people were going to want to know our story. As a journalist he felt that they would be interested in knowing how we found the place, when we came here and why. Rather alarmingly he pointed out that, because of this adventure, we were going to be regarded as something out of the ordinary and of some interest.

Inevitably we would be asked what made us do it, how long had the idea been in our minds and, once the interrogators discovered that we had not been together from the word Go, how and where we met. How right he was and time after time we listened patiently as the same questions were asked. Initially it was a little frustrating as we wanted to know about our guests and tried to get in a question or two of our own here and there but the subject always returned to our little story.

It was only natural that if people had decided to come and stay with us they would like to know how we had set about it all. Although many hundreds of folk have succeeded in doing what we were attempting to do, every story was a little different. I thought of the massive undertaking that Jerry Baker had set himself down the road and chuckled at the thought of how some of our guests would have found life there or what Archie and Sarah Shaw had taken on in the Gers. For all we knew our visitors might have had a ghastly experience with British hosts elsewhere and wanted to reassure themselves that Bosc Lebat was not another minefield.

We were not rushed off our feet by visitors that first summer. While we welcomed the extra income, we had to keep chipping away at numerous chores about the place, in addition to which we were still learning fast. We had to settle into some sort of daily routine whereby we could get ourselves organised first and then turn our attention to the guests. It meant a very early start as Tristan had to get away to school soon after seven.

We bought him a little *mobilette* to give him a measure of independence and, once fed and watered, he would clamber aboard the bike with his mass of homework in a large bag on his back and struggle up the hill behind the house, en route for Lavaur. In the evenings we would keep an ear open for the sound of the approaching bike which told us that he had returned safely home. Even now the sound of a little *mobilette* speeding by makes Rachel catch her breath.

Tristan settled remarkably well into the routine and was on course to move up to the *lycée* to do his *Baccalauréat*. From there he had decided that he would like to go on to university in the UK. We knew already that a good pass in the *Baccalauréat* was acceptable to most British universities, thus he had a goal ahead of him, he appeared to have had found his feet and was happy with his lot.

We had asked the guests that, unless they particularly wanted an early start, they should appear for breakfast at any time after eight-thirty. This was popular and meant that they could then get themselves ready to leave the house for their day's activities at a decent hour.

Some of our guests arrived highly organised and knew exactly what they wanted to do whilst others came with only the vaguest notion of what the area was like or what they might get up to during their stay. This made life difficult all round and we were left wondering if we should just leave them to get on with it or wade in like some inane travel agent extolling the virtues of everything within striking distance.

On one occasion we had a couple of splendid elderly Belgians in the house who had gone to the other extreme. The dining room became the operations centre and we would listen spellbound as the old boy briefed up his wife on every twist and turn of the day's activities – timetable, wet and dry weather programmes, meals – the lot. She sat there taking it all for as long as she could when she would turn up her deaf aid so that a piercing whistle brought the instructions to a halt. But we had to give them their due, the Tarn and surrounding Departments were toured to death and they left knowing more about this corner of France than the local French.

At the end of breakfast I would hover, discretely within earshot, to see if help was needed. Many of those who had not given the day a thought were often grateful for a few ideas. Easy enough if everyone in the party wanted to do the same thing but when one wanted to disappear off into the mountains and the other chose to lie by the pool, I trod warily fearful of getting drawn into family disputes.

The worst problem by far was dealing with inclement weather. Morale of even the stoutest hearts would sag when the clouds gathered and we would be subjected to uncharitable comments about our local climate. The weather in the Tarn is good – usually very good – but we do get our fair share of rain which is needed to keep the countryside in such a green and pleasant state. The rich farmland and vineyards are amongst the Tarn's great attractions which, together with Languedoc and Gascony, is renowned for the cuisine based on the local agriculture. Quite simply, one cannot have the one without the other.

Sometime later in the year a party of six elderly Canadians booked in for two weeks. Not in the least deterred by the autumn rains they set about their holiday in a businesslike manner setting out day after day to seek out the best wine and food, returning in the evening after one good meal before going out again for a second. Samples of the goods that had made their mark together with an inordinate amount of excellent wine were brought into the house for us to try. As the bottles emptied so the tales of life in the Canadian wilderness and frozen north became ever more bizarre and improbable, but that was their way and they left us happily, threatening a return visit.

However, our first summer here was quite the worst weather we have experienced and we were subjected to some memorable, torrential downpours that revealed the location of every cracked and broken tile, every leaking gutter and blocked drain. But, throughout it all, our early guests seemed to enjoy our hospitality and went on their way apparently content with their holiday. It proved to be every bit as much fun as we had dared hope, several have returned on a number of occasions whilst others have recommended us to their friends.

Quite one of the most memorable early visits was made by a wonderful little old lady who I had known in Winchester. Mildred, now well into her eighties, would, at the drop of a hat, look back over an incredible life. A name-dropper par excellence she would count, amongst her host of friends and admirers, Errol Flynn, Noel Coward, a very senior member of the Spanish Royal household plus a whole gaggle of others about whom she spun many a fanciful yarn.

She was also an accomplished artist and had come all this way to present to yet another past admirer a beautiful painting of a French cockerel standing rampant in the rick yard. Just why she insisted on handing over this particular painting she steadfastly refused to reveal.

At her request we arranged for the ceremony to take place at a well-known local restaurant and the following morning, Charity, her niece recounted how Mildred and her beau of all those years ago had tried in vain to rekindle the flames but, whilst youthful passions might not have been in order, they held the diners and staff enthralled with stories of how life was really lived and who did all the living. She was with us for two more days before, in a state of nervous exhaustion, we managed to get her into the car still chattering away.

One day in August we sensed that an unusually heavy thunderstorm was brewing. Throughout the afternoon the air got heavier and the heavens finally opened around six in the evening when more than two inches of rain cascaded down in less than half an hour. There were numerous reports of severe flooding across the south of France and northern Spain. We were unharmed but the unfinished landscaping around the swimming pool was devastated.

I had laid a land drain around the edge of the pool terracing, covering it with a deep layer of large pebbles and stones, to cope with such an eventuality. What I had failed to do, though, was to make any allowances for the soil that had been exposed by the excavations of the pool site. The downpour had simply churned the friable loam into a porridge which had then flowed down the banks like lava into, over and around the stones and terracing, stopping just short of the pool itself.

Heavy clay mud and large stones well mixed are not moved easily and there were tons of this melange which all but drove us to our knees as, for the next two days, we cleared and cleaned the site. The steep banks around the pool are now terraced with old railway sleepers and we have planted out the area with Mediterranean plants and shrubs. It is a hard way to learn about landscaping but the plants and terracing are an attractive combination and, thus far, the banks have held secure.

We had been warned on many occasions that, sooner or later, we would be put to the test – somebody would arrive and things would go wrong. It was an alarming thought but there was absolutely nothing we could do about it other than soldier on and take life as it came. Early in the year we had taken a call from a lady in Norfolk who introduced herself first as a yoga teacher but later as a hypnotherapist. Would we, she enquired, be prepared to do a deal on the *gîte* together with rooms in the house at the same time?

The plan was for her and her assistant to stay in the house with us whilst her patients – clients to her – stayed in the *gîte*. She wanted peace and quiet so that they could get on with whatever it was that hypnotherapists do. It sounded harmless enough to us and we agreed to her proposal. At this stage I was warned by the good lady that, during the daily sessions with her clients, there might be sounds of chanting and raised voices. We thought about this and, still unaware of what it was all about, gave the go ahead on the understanding that the other guests were not disturbed.

At the time we had a couple staying in the house with their daughter and a school friend. Back for their third holiday with us, Phil and Angela Evans came from Kent where Phil ran a flourishing herbal medicine business. He knew a great deal about the mysteries of alternative medicines and warned us, with a wry smile, that things might get interesting.

The therapists eventually showed up with their clients as planned and settled into their accommodation. I had begun to read up about hypnotherapy and gathered that the process involved taking the patient back to the point in life where the problem began. Once this point had been determined the remedial treatment commenced. What I did not know anything about was how the troubled souls were taken back to the point in question.

I had given the party the use of our big barns where, so I was told, conditions were perfect for the treatment. Bosc Lebat was going about its daily routine, Bernard our trusty postman had just delivered the morning mail to the barn, when the curtain went up. I think we all made an honest effort to get on with our own business and leave our guests to their escapades but gradually we became aware of the sound of feet shuffling across the wooden floor of the barn loft. Slowly the sound increased until a rhythmic stamping accompanied the shuffling – something akin to a Maori Haka.

'Sounds like Zulu warriors,' quipped Phil. After a time the chanting started, followed by some loud shouts and finally some ear-splitting, blood-curdling screams. At this point all the lights fused, Phil's daughter and friend went pale, even the dogs looked uneasy. Rachel asked me to go and find out what on earth had happened.

My immediate reaction was that somebody had been electrocuted so I rushed into the barn and up the stairs expecting the worst. Previously I had promised that we would leave them well alone so that they could get on with their affairs, yet here I was bursting in upon them to be greeted by a scene in which they were all sitting or lying on the floor, less one person who was crouched in a corner sobbing uncontrollably. The hypnotherapist rounded on me angrily, accusing me of breaking my word, telling me that I had interrupted and spoiled an important part of the treatment.

Their morning session over, I had no option but to tell the leader of the party that she too had broken her word in that the house and guests had been subjected to the sounds of the ritual, some of which were quite alarming. Somehow things were going to have to be rearranged. Sadly this was not the happiest of associations. The point I found most troublesome was that the patients or clients seemed such a happy lot when down at the pool or around the gardens. One or two were perhaps a little unsure of themselves but it seemed extraordinary that they had to go through all this to be helped on their way.

I learned later that this type of practice is becoming more popular but there have been one or two widely publicised instances when it has all gone badly wrong. We never were to find out what benefits the shuffling and chanting, the screams and tears brought to those who came all this way but decided that alternative medicines such as this were not for Bosc Lebat. Should we get any such enquiries in the future we would seek Phil's advice as to what might be in store for us and our guests.

A short time after this I received a call from an old army chum. I had known Ted for years, in fact we had served together in the Radfan. There, Captain Ted Ware had been a helicopter pilot, a member of the squadron that supported us on all our operations in the mountains. Sometimes under fire, often flying amongst the ragged peaks at dusk, or even in complete darkness, their support was magnificent and they lived with us in the forward base at Habilayn some seventy-five miles to the north of Aden.

Ted was a dapper man, always dressed immaculately for the occasion in crisp, starched fatigues, a small cravat around his neck; he looked quite out of place amongst the rest of us covered in war paint and festooned with weapons and grenades. Ted, however, suffered from bad gout and used to appear at briefings limping heavily, supported by a malacca cane, invariably calling out to us all, 'Morning chaps, sorry I'm a bit late. Just been to see the doc. Don't worry, everything's fine. Now what's on for today?'

'Just don't get brought down in the mountains dressed like that,' my troop sergeant would growl. 'You'll need more than a ruddy walking stick and fancy silk necktie if that lot up there get their hands on yer.' Once in the machine Ted became the complete professional. Flying low, fast and with amazing skill, he and the others never let us down. Later, under fire, he flew into a major contact in the Wadi Taim, to lift me and the other casualties out and took us down to the forward hospital. I had a great affection for him and now here he was again. It would be tremendous to see him.

Ted lived life to the full and time had not dampened his high spirits or his wild Irish ways. Shortly before we left England we met again after many years. It was a good party and we chatted about old times. Ted introduced me to his wife, Jenny, and although an attractive enough woman, I feared that she knew her man well and was keeping him on a tight leash. I told him that I was to leave the Army soon, explaining what we were planning to do and, at party's end, we went our separate ways.

Now he was asking me if we had a nice room for a weekend's break. 'You know, a bit of peace and quiet, away from it all.'

'Double or single?' I enquired.

'Double of course, with a good, big comfy bed,' was the reply.

'Great,' I cried, 'Jenny coming as well?'

The short silence that followed said it all. No, Ted would be coming along with someone else – nudge, nudge, wink, wink. The old dog had not changed a bit so we prepared ourselves accordingly. The evening flight from London got into Toulouse late and Rachel had gone to bed by the time Ted and lady friend drew up at the house.

No sooner inside the door than he unashamedly began to attack the bottle of Duty Free he had just given me. Wrestling what was left from his grasp I took him up to the one remaining guest room we had available. 'Here you are, you old rogue,' I announced opening the door and waving him in.

'Bloody marvellous,' he enthused, 'this is great, Paddy. I'll let Carol sleep in here. Where am I going?'

My jaw dropped and I stared at him in disbelief, 'You're in there too, you bloody old rogue. Just because you've cocked it up on the plane or whatever, it's too late now to start thinking about separate rooms and all that.'

'Ah, I see. Oh, all right. Well, look, no problem. I'm sure things will be OK.'

'Damn right they will,' I muttered, 'And if they're not, we don't want any roaring and yelling, waking the whole house up. It's long gone midnight now.'

'No sweat, Paddy, you know me. I'll handle things. See you in the morning.'

How Ted got out of that one we never knew. As soon as they had gone upstairs I shut down the house and beat a hasty retreat before the good Carol was appraised of the situation and took whatever action she saw fit. Poor old Ted – win some, lose some! Breakfast the following morning, so Rachel reported, was a tense affair. However they went off together for the day in good spirits after Ted confided in me that he had spent a terrible night trying to sleep in the bath. The following evening we put Carol into the Students' Quarter behind two doors that she could lock if she felt threatened.

I doubt that Ted ever got his money's worth that weekend but gradually the sun loungers at the pool got closer together as the weekend wore on and Ted got everyone laughing with his outrageous banter before they left for London still jockeying for position.

# CHAPTER XII

# Tales of Pool and Garden

*A betting man. The Pool. Andre and Tanya de Beauville.*
*Fraught guests. November 11th – On Parade again!*

Our first short season was drawing to a close and we were beginning to look at a winter of consolidation and a hefty work programme. There was still lots to be done and we had achieved precious little once the guests had arrived. Looking back we felt it had been fun. We had survived the odd hiccup but, as we had hoped, the vast majority of those who came and stayed were a delight to have around. Rather than fussing them or pandering to every little whim or fancy, we decided to let them do very much as they wished but within a few clearly defined parameters.

Neither of us smoked and both found the smell of stale tobacco obnoxious so we asked our visitors to refrain from smoking upstairs. Most were delighted with this arrangement but it is unbelievable how sensitive smokers can be when asked to curb their habit so that it does not impose on those who do not share their addiction to the weed. On one particular occasion a strong smoker laced her reply to our modest request with heavy sarcasm asking pointedly if she would be permitted to have a cigarette in the middle of the field beyond the pool.

Such moments are difficult. The first reaction to such a jibe is to tell them to pack their bags and push off if they really do feel that way about it. But that is the very last resort and on such occasions you have to be quick on your feet to defuse the situation, placate whoever is up in arms, whilst at the same time, try and ensure that one of our few house rules is observed.

That first summer we offered to do lunches for a moderate price. This proved to be wildly popular, but we soon found why this was so and that we had made a very bad mistake. Many guests like to potter off for a couple of hours in the morning and then return for a while. If lunch is on offer then so much the better – the temptation of a cold spread under the trees washed down with a bottle or two of chilled wine is difficult to resist.

If they could then get away without having to drive after such a treat then the afternoon plans are scrapped in favour of a snooze in a deck chair or on the bed. Lunches on holiday are something to be savoured rather than hurried.

Rather alarmingly we found that, no sooner had we finished our morning chores, than lunch was on the go, after which there was the evening meal to prepare. Not only had our precious few moments of peace and quiet in the early afternoon disappeared but, whilst the world and his wife later slept off the effects of a good lunch, preparations for the evening meal became something of a gallop.

There were occasions when the midday meal would take a different course. Once a family from Yorkshire was staying and as lunch approached Alan began to show concern for the time of day in England and asked if we knew anything about the weather in Yorkshire. Somewhat baffled by this performance we started lunch and were well into the meal when Alan again looked at his watch.

'Would you mind if I made a call to Yorkshire?' he asked. Wondering if this had anything to do with his query about the weather at home I waved him towards the office. A few moments later he reappeared, grinning but looking a trifle concerned.

'You look a wee bit worried about something,' I said, 'Is everything alright?'

'Paddy, I'll let you know in ten minutes. I've just put fifteen hundred quid on a horse running at York.' I filled his glass, mine also and followed him into the office where his cheerful expression told me that the voice on the phone had brought good news.

'Well, that's paid for the holiday – let me buy the next bottle.' Then, turning to me, he asked, 'Paddy, tell me. What would you have done if I had lost and couldn't pay you?'

'God knows! Called for double or quits, I suppose.' What it must be like to win that amount in one go, or indeed lose it, I could not imagine. We laughed at the thought of it and set about enjoying a rare bottle of Alan's St Joseph under the trees with the others.

Rachel worked herself to the bone on these occasions and it was obvious that, without the necessary help, we could not keep this going. The white flag was waved and we now invite the guests to go into town and get themselves a picnic, bring it back here and have it as and when they like in the gardens. We are happy to chill the wine, provide all the implements, rugs, tables and chairs. It is a successful formula, the more so as the picnic is but a short step away from the pool, the deck chairs or the bed.

There is one small corner of Bosc Lebat which is sacred and that is the kitchen. It is Rachel's domain and hers alone in which intruders are less than welcome. Should they be foolish enough to push their luck and cross this particular threshold early in the day, at a time when we are about our business, then they are deep in enemy territory. At this hour the lady of Bosc Lebat might, on occasions, be caught without her make-up and with her hair in curlers. Most ladies of the house would rather be found stark naked than in such a state and Rachel is no exception. The kitchen is strictly her territory and to intrude at any time, let alone at an unseemly hour, is tempting fate.

One problem we have yet to overcome is the fact that any wine our guests purchase and wish to keep chilled is kept in the fridge behind the kitchen which lives down the corridor next to our quarters. Although we are at pains to ask them when they want it, some choose to save us trouble and one of the party, usually the lady, sneaks through in search of the said bottles. This is harmless enough but occasionally, after a morning of particularly hard labour, we too choose to take an afternoon nap when we simply strip off and crash out on the bed in the heat of the afternoon, dead to the world.

Should a lady guest choose to penetrate the nether regions of Bosc Lebat, no matter how honourable her intentions, I am afraid that she risks stumbling across her hosts. On the very rare occasions that such a confrontation has taken place the intruder has invariably owned up later amidst hoots of laughter all round and her own demure blushes. They never let on as to the cause of the blushes but such an intrusion is never repeated.

The pool produced an interesting little problem of its own. Throughout the summer months it is, without doubt, the centre of social life at Bosc Lebat. Almost everybody goes down there to cool off at some point during the day and towards late afternoon most seem to gather there. We allowed for this eventuality by ordering a good size pool and putting in a large area of terracing so there would be plenty of room for everyone.

The difficulty is that house guests and *gîte* tenants tend to differ somewhat. Most of our house guests are middle aged or elderly folk and like to take a quiet swim followed by a peaceful hour or so by the pool with a good book or the newspapers before coming back to the house. The *gîte* is very much a family scene and the youngsters are raring to go and let their hair down. Once they see the pool they are straining at the leash.

Children are children the world over and love to make a noise in the water. The two most likely candidates for this are teenage boys who seem hell bent on yelling their heads off whilst displacing as much water as possible, and little girls who like standing in the shallow end, screaming shrilly. All well and good if they are the only ones there, but, come late afternoon, the potential for confrontation is considerable.

Colonel Thunder is unlikely to be amused when his copy of *The Times* is blasted out of his hands by a misdirected football, neither does Lady Camilla take kindly to being battered and bombarded as she proceeds sedately up and down the pool doing her daily dozen. On the other hand parents are not amused at the thought of their little darlings being hog tied and muzzled, cowering in fear of their very lives should they so much as utter a sound.

A delicate balancing act is the answer when everyone is asked to consider how others like to enjoy themselves. I was worried that we would ever be able to strike a balance but it seems to have worked. Somehow our guests have managed and we have yet to return the shattered copy of *The Times*, assist a shell-shocked senior citizen from the water or release miscreant children from muzzles and leg irons.

We ask all our guests if they would be kind enough to leave the pool free for us between the hours of one and three in the afternoon. Most people are having lunch at this time or would have gone out for the day. Rachel and I go down there for a quiet couple of hours, a swim and a bit of sun before taking up the reins once more. Occasionally, when no one is around we steal an extra hour.

Once we had a very attractive, curvaceous young musician staying with us to help out with the chores and practise with Rachel. One afternoon, after a session of tedious redecorating, we realised that we had the place to ourselves so we went down to the pool, stripped right off and luxuriated in the water before lying in the afternoon sun. A short while later, whilst the girls lay basking in all their glory, I slipped back into the water and began to clean the edges of the pool.

Suddenly I heard a polite, if somewhat theatrical, little cough followed by a giggle coming from the direction of the rose pergola. 'Now, I've caught you,' cried the voice. 'What are you all up to?' There, looking as pretty as a picture, was Tanya, the lovely Philippine wife of Andre de Beauville whose parents live in the magnificent Chateau La Verdarie a few kilometres up the road.

'Yes, you've certainly got me. What would you like me to do about it?' I called back but by this time the girls, realising that someone was about, had put towels around themselves and walked over. 'Put this on and behave yourself,' chuckled Rachel, throwing me a towel, as she and Charlotte went across to Tanya.

'Do you all behave like this around here?' Tanya asked us. She went on to explain that she had decided to walk over from the Chateau and whilst on the way took a short cut along a track through the woods. There she passed a middle-aged woman, body burned nut brown, clad just as the Almighty had decreed, out walking with her large dog. We admitted that this was not exactly the norm and she had chanced upon a rare moment at Bosc Lebat. The four of us walked slowly up to the house.

Tanya and Andre had become good friends of ours and although they lived in Paris, came down from time to time to see the family and, whenever they did this, would call us up and come over for tea or a drink. We had been up to stay with them in their lovely house set back from the Champs-Elysées in a quiet street close to the British Embassy. They spoiled us dreadfully and we were always delighted to see them at Bosc Lebat.

A few minutes later a rather battered, very senior Peugeot came to a halt at the top of the drive and Andre emerged. Andre was, quite simply, born fifty years too late. Quiet, dignified and blessed with impeccable manners and an old world charm that did full justice to even his long pedigree, Andre was straight out of a P.G. Wodehouse novel. Dressed immaculately as always, his light dun-coloured tropical suit, silk shirt and tie together with panama hat and silver-topped stick, clashed incongruously with our towels, sun cream and flip-flops.

Tanya, too, was beautifully turned out. Dressed in bright clothes and wearing exquisite perfume, her tiny and delicate figure always reminded me of a little butterfly. She chuckled as Andre walked slowly across the lawn. Coming up to Rachel, he took her hand, raised it gently towards his lips and, without taking his eyes from hers, said quietly, 'Rachel, my dear, how simply delightful to see you again.' She received him with all

*'Rachel, my dear, how simply delightful to see you again.'*

the dignity she could muster, hair wet from the pool, left hand behind her back holding in place the precariously supported towel.

Andre turned next to Charlotte whose bronzed, fulsome and even more dangerously uncovered figure would have drawn the attention of all but the most courteous and disciplined of men. He looked her straight in the eye and, as I introduced them, inclined his head slightly towards her hand and murmured, 'Quite enchanting.' Finally he looked across at me, one eyebrow slightly cocked, a roguish grin from ear to ear. Taking my hand he enquired, 'Paddy, my dear good fellow, how are you? The ravages of life still bearing down heavily, I see.'

Tanya and Andre made a wonderful couple. She hailed from the very height of Philippine society, her aristocratic family stretching far back into the country's history. Beautifully educated, well connected, always gorgeously dressed and immensely rich, Tanya did not want for anything. Until she got married and left her parental home she had never even suffered the indignity of washing or setting her own hair, countless maids forever being in attendance.

Now, with Andre, a man of property, they toured the world together following the opera circuit, wintering at Gstaad and holidaying in the Orient. Neither had the faintest idea how the rest of us struggled along in our grubby little worlds. Andre looked upon our business at Bosc Lebat with genuine horror and concern. 'How can you possibly do this, dear boy? All those dreadful people around you the whole time!'

'Oh, it's not that bad, Andre. We pick and choose as carefully as we can – retired officers, old school chums, that sort of thing.'

'You English have been so clever to hang on to your class system,' he mused. 'Here in France we have none of that any longer. It all went years ago, and Heaven knows what you would have turning up on your door step if you advertised here.' It was marvellous stuff, nobody lived like that these days, but here they were and it was wonderful to see them.

Rachel and Charlotte appeared a few minutes later, now clad more securely, carrying trays of tea. Andre delighted in Rachel's blend of Earl

Grey and her walnut cakes, one of which was now cut into small slices, together with all the bits and pieces for the tea on the tray. After enquiring about our business the subject turned to Paris. When, they wanted to know, would we be next able to join them?

The mere thought of it was a treat and we both often recalled how Andre used to take us to breakfast with him at the Cafe Flore in Paris St Germain. Here, he would be met by his waiter, be taken to his usual table where he would be served with two fresh eggs boiled for four minutes exactly, toast with Dundee marmalade and, of course, Earl Grey gently brewed. Usually he would sit there alone, studying *Le Figaro* and *The Times* while the day gently unfolded itself for him.

It was a wonderful idea and, had we been able, we would have gone like a shot but the daily routine at Bosc Lebat kept us from straying into this rarefied atmosphere. Before they took their leave, we promised we would try – and we meant it. As the old car ground slowly up the hill Charlotte shook her head, 'I can't believe it. I just didn't think that there were people left like that!'

It did not take us long to realise that a large number of our guests had been working away under considerable strain and intense pressure in the office, the City or wherever before escaping down here for a break. Whether they belonged to the ranks of the highly successful who were forever driving themselves to go that extra mile or amongst the less fortunate who were having to drive themselves just as hard simply to survive, many people arrived in a pretty dreadful state and were absolutely whacked. At first we were not too sure how to handle such situations. When people are very tired they are very rarely themselves. We had no idea that, under all the twitching and tension, there was somebody else hidden away who was going to take a day or two to emerge.

One such couple arrived from the north of England. He was a very high-powered head of a number of companies, and his wife had forced him away for a break. He had piloted his own plane into Toulouse – a task unlikely to steady nerves already jangling – hired a large car, raced out here and pulled up at the front door in a shower of gravel.

He leapt from the driver's seat, rushed past the reception committee to the boot of the car, extracted two large suitcases, staggered up to us and, without pausing to introduce himself, cried out, 'OK, let's go!' Rachel and I, hands extended in greeting, stared in bewilderment and all we could do was to say soothingly, 'My dear good chap, there's nowhere to go. You have arrived. Put those things down and come and have a cup of tea.'

Admittedly this was an exception but the message was clear in that for two days at least people need to unwind in their own ways and adjust to the peace and quiet, far removed from the workplace. We have learned to develop a considerable sympathy for our fellow beings who have been running on the treadmill for months on end and are eternally grateful that we are not caught up in that mad world of constant pressure. If we are able to ease the strain and send them home refreshed for the battles ahead then we have done our bit.

Every summer our orchards at Bosc Lebat produce a marvellous variety of fresh fruit. From the red, black and yellow cherries in early May to the figs in late September, we and our guests are spoilt for choice. Rachel picks what she can and makes mountains of jam and chutney but her best efforts make little impact on the harvest and I all but march our guests to whichever trees are bearing fruit at the time and order them to pick as much as possible.

Even this is not enough and we ring around our friends telling them to come over with baskets and to help themselves. It is a wonderful sight watching the parents up ladders and perched precariously in the trees picking as fast as they can while, underneath, the children are eating the contents of the baskets almost as fast, small faces and sticky little hands covered in fruit juice.

Apart from the fruit we have thirty young walnut trees and towards the end of September the nuts ripen and begin to fall. October is the busy month and I am sometimes out in the orchards for hours on end collecting the harvest. The nuts first ripen in their pods on the trees which later swell and burst open, releasing the fresh young nuts to fall on the ground. If the weather remains dry some of the nuts remain in their pods and, unless there is a good wind, they have to be knocked down either by youngsters shinning up the branches or with long sticks – hence the wise old English ditty: 'Your wife, your dog and walnut tree, the more you beat them the better they be!'

We sell the nuts on to friends and members of the *chasse*. Some of the local restaurants take more and the remainder, apart from the ones Rachel keeps back for cakes and salads, go to a local retailer. They are particularly popular with one of our favourite restaurants and on occasions I time my delivery with a meal there. No money changes hands, I simply hand twenty-five kilos of walnuts to Le Patron in return for an excellent meal and an enjoyable evening out.

Autumn came and with it a spell of glorious weather – long overdue after the rains earlier in the year. November 11th happens to be Rachel's birthday and it is also Armistice Day. France takes the whole business of remembering very seriously having lost so many countless thousands in the two great wars. Shortly before Armistice Sunday we received a formal invitation from the Mairie asking us to attend the service in the local church followed by the Act of Remembrance at the war memorial, the whole morning finishing with a *vin d'honneur* at the village school.

I studied the invitation closely and had a strong suspicion that it was to be nothing less than a formal parade which demanded dark suit, regimental tie, medals, bowler hat, umbrella et al and I was right. I had all the bits and pieces tucked away somewhere but when it came to the bowler and brolly I paused. This, I thought, might look a bit out of place in the midst of the small French rural community. I did not wish to draw attention to myself but felt that I should represent the old country in good order and correctly turned out. I considered the various options and decided that most of the *anciens* on parade would be wearing their old regimental berets so I dug out my old beige regimental beret, cast aside the brolly and mingled with the other veterans.

It was a wise decision and I took my place with hardly a second glance coming my way. The service was very similar to our own in that the standards of the Sociétés des Anciens were marched in under escort and placed at the altar. The service was lead by the town band who then marched in front of the congregation down the short route to the memorial where the whole community was gathered around in a large semi-circle.

The ceremony began with the youngest children of the village stepping forward and laying, not wreaths, but small posies of flowers at the base of the memorial. This was followed by a number of short orations, one from the Maire, another from a representative of the Consul General of the Tarn and a third by an *ancien combatant* selected by the Maire.

This year a retired nun had been asked to give this particular oration. Stooped with age and walking slowly with a stick, the tiny figure stepped out from behind the ranks of *anciens* and stood diminutive beside the other speakers. When her turn came she faced the assembled community and began to speak in a strong voice filled with emotion. I looked closely at her and saw that two of the medals on her breast were the Legion d'Honneur and, even more surprisingly, the red and green stripes of Le Croix de Guerre.

I learned later that she had been a young nurse in North Africa during the War and had been caught up in the worst of the fighting there. Now in her eighties she harked back to those terrible times and exhorted us all to remember the sacrifices made by those who were so young and whose names were inscribed on the memorial behind her.

As she concluded her voice rose as she cried out '*Vive la Republique, Vive la Republique!*' at which point the band struck up the evocative La Marseillaise. Here, the whole village – men, women and children – straightened their backs, placed their right hands over their hearts and sung for all they were worth, tears in many an eye, whilst we, *les anciens*, threw up the very best of our salutes.

It was a remarkable gesture of spontaneous patriotism, the tiny farming community demonstrating a great depth of feeling for the occasion. As the last notes of the anthem faded away the gathering fell silent, each one alone with his or her thoughts, until the Maire lead the way to the little school where we all tucked into a splendid *vin d'honneur*. It was a most impressive occasion in which the whole community gathered to remember the supreme sacrifice made by the young men of Massac-Seran all those years ago.

# CHAPTER XIII

# Times Get Serious

*Late summer and autumn. More local artisans.*
*Our times with Nick the builder.*

As the season drew towards its close and the evenings began to shorten we looked around at what needed to be done, organising the tasks into a long list of priorities. 'The Essentials' headed the list, competing fiercely for the Number One spot, whilst further down lay the things we would like to get done if time and finances permitted. These we called 'The Desirables' and in the first few years we never got down that far, in fact even The Essentials changed their order of priority when some problem or other suddenly became a crisis.

I had long since realised I was no handyman. I was an extremely hard-working and capable labourer but whenever anything remotely technical or complicated came along I bowed to the inevitable and sought help. We were now distinctly wary of British workmen and had drawn up a list of local artisans whom we had got to know and on whom we intended to call for major works. It therefore came as something of a surprise when we heard through some French friends that an Englishman was working in and around Lavaur.

My initial reaction was to warn our friends to steer well clear of the character but, time and again, I was assured that he worked on his own and would not, therefore, be drawing attention to himself. He did not touch electrics or complicated plumbing and his work was extremely good. In fact he was in demand amongst the French community and there was a waiting list for his services. I went along to our neighbours to see some of his work and it was indeed of high quality. His name was Nick and I set out to track him down, promising my fellow countrymen one more chance.

I put a call through to him and he came out to Bosc Lebat to introduce himself. Many years previously Nick had been in the Army, rising to the dizzy height of Lance Corporal in a famous infantry regiment, known as the Royal Green Jackets, with whom he had been for six years and which I knew well. He had left the Army and gone into the building trade, working initially on the huge cooling towers of the power stations in the north of England and Scotland. After some years there he had met his present girlfriend and had decided to try his luck in France.

Nick was permanently cheerful and I immediately warmed to him. We discussed what had to be done around the place. As he had been in Lavaur for a few years he knew most of the artisans and, were we to do anything complicated, he knew who to engage. He lived in a tiny terraced house in Lavaur's old quarter and it was galling to think that we had only found each other now rather than a year earlier when we were having all sorts of problems and he had been desperately looking for work. Now he had his hands full but agreed to make a start on our projects in the New Year.

Towards the end of the year we sat back and took stock of the situation. The business was now up and running, indeed the advertisements for next season were starting to bring in enquiries. The financial situation remained tight, however, and Rachel ran the accounts with strict control, forcing us both to account for every Franc spent – each and every payment was noted in the fly leaf of the cheque book whether it had been made by cheque, plastic or cash. It was the only way under the circumstances.

French banks have an aggressive and uncompromising attitude towards those who allow themselves to become overdrawn. Quite simply no one is allowed to get into this situation without permission and woe betide those who do. We were told that there have been occasions when the miscreants have been taken to court for such a hideous offence and when found guilty of the dastardly crime have been sent down for a spell.

The plus side to this rather draconian attitude is that the bank card is accepted everywhere without any fuss about being invited to prove one's identity or prove there is actually something in the account. Everybody knows that those who fall foul of the system are in for the high jump and this makes life a lot easier at the cash desks.

We did not appreciate this fully at first and on one occasion, while waiting for the pensions to come through, went into the red just as one would at home. It was a matter of only a few Francs but the balloon went up and we were summoned to the bank without delay to explain ourselves. All was well and our good friend Anne Marie came to the rescue but we learned, from that moment on, to keep a very close watch on our funds.

It is a tedious business but we decided against running the risk of being called back into the headmaster's study and being reminded, with much ceremony, that zero in the account means zero in the account. This is a point conveniently overlooked by UK banks who choose to sit back and wait for their customers to get into all sorts of a financial mess before hooking them on to fearful interest rates for their overdrafts and loans.

Christmas came and went, the New Year was seen in, and before long Nick came up and we began work on the large room to the right of the front door which was to become our drawing room. We had cleared the room of furniture and Nick studied what had to be done. He saw in an instant that the problem which had so nearly done for the piano came from the old tiled floor.

'You are going to have to lose this,' he said, tapping the floor with his foot. 'These old tiles are like sponges and I bet you anything you like that under here is a whole load of old rubble and then clay soil. Nothing after that – no foundations, nothing!' He caught the worried look on my face and added hurriedly, 'Don't worry too much, the place has been standing for three hundred years and isn't going to collapse now. That's the way they used to do things here.'

The walls, so he thought, were fine, as was the ceiling, apart from where he suggested we should lower it a bit and insulate the area in between, leaving the massive redwood beams exposed. Against the hall wall was the site of an old open fireplace. After examining the chimney and flues Nick suggested a wood-burning stove.

'An open fire is very pretty, but most of the heat goes straight up the chimney. This is a big room and you will need all the heat you can get come winter. Added to which a wood burner is that much cleaner – none of the ash drifting around the room.' I agreed, as did Rachel who was called in to give her final nod of approval to these suggestions.

So, to work we went. My first task was to get hold of forty-five square metres of top-quality pine flooring, treat it and then stain it to match the beams. Nick, meanwhile, had attacked the floor. One by one the old tiles came away and these we put to one side. Underneath was the rubble he guessed would be there, and there were tons of the stuff. A skip was brought in and for the next few days we sweated away.

Suddenly Nick gave a shout 'Hey, come and look at this!' We gathered around a circular indenture in the rubble where stones of a different sort had been laid. 'Know what this is? It's an old well and its right under the spot where Rachel put her piano. No wonder it didn't like it in here. There you are, that's what's done the damage.'

It was an amazing and tragic coincidence. During our first and very wet winter the water table must have risen right up until it was just under or even touching the old tiles. These had soaked up the moisture which had then escaped into the atmosphere of the room right under the Bechstein. Small wonder the piano had been soaking wet.

Once the rubble had been cleared away we capped the old well, laid a thick concrete base to the floor followed by a polythene membrane and then the wooden battens for the floor. Finally the floor itself was laid and, once this had been polished up a couple of times the room was ready. Nick then fitted the wood-burning stove, tiled the foot of the walls and went outside to lay the remainder of the old tiles as a long line of steps from the front lawn down to the pool. He told us to try out the stove before he went. We did just this and nearly lost the house as a result.

Wood-burning stoves are remarkably efficient, the heating comes not only from the stove itself but from the chimney pipe which gets so hot that it burns to the touch. We were sitting by the fire admiring the handiwork when Rachel asked quietly, 'What's that mark on the wall behind the pipe?'

I went over to have a look and, to my horror, saw that the wallpaper we had put on two days previously was now smouldering. We let the fire die down and Nick was recalled. He looked at the wall behind the stove, disappeared into the hall then returned saying, 'Look, it's my guess that there is a lovely old brick and stone wall underneath this lot. If there is, I can do you a smashing exposed feature here. What do you think? Shall I have a stab with the pick?'

We thought the room had been finished and had cleaned up all the mess; now this. But something had to be done so we crossed our fingers and gave him the go-ahead. The head of the pick slammed into the paper and plaster. Gently Nick eased it back and a chunk fell to the floor revealing a large grey stone. 'There we are, my beauty, just look at that,' he crowed. We moved the furniture away and Nick got to work gently teasing out great slabs of plaster exposing a marvellous old wall, an old doorway and some parts of old beams. These now make up the wall behind the stove giving the room an added dimension.

As the autumn and winter wore on we became aware of some problems with the *gîte* – legacies of the earlier British builders. Leaks began to appear in the plumbing and the wood-burning stove that we had installed was not drawing well, neither were the rooms heating up. In fact the *gîte* was a cold place in winter, a point not lost on the tenants who were becoming increasingly uncomfortable. I mentioned all this to Nick who, although unable to do the work himself, agreed to have a look and make some suggestions.

His first port of call was the stove and the chimney. Years ago he had been a spiderman on cooling towers and pylons, working aloft at dizzying heights in all weathers. The *gîte* chimney was no problem for him so, calling for me to follow, he got out of the skylight and onto the roof of the *manoir* where he ran nimbly along the steep ridge, down the other side and across the barn roof to the *gîte*. At this point he jumped up on to the top of the chimney stack calling again for me to follow.

'You have to be joking!' I shouted, wobbling precariously on the ridge tiles, the broad expanse of our valley now fully exposed to my gaze and a long way beneath me.

'What's up, grandad? I thought you had been in the Paras or something like that.'

'Just shut up and get on with what I'm paying you for,' I muttered, inching my way along to the base of the chimney which I grabbed and embraced with both arms.

After apologising for taking the mickey from the old buffer, Nick got us back to terra firma where he explained that the whole chimney needed to be resleeved. He knew of an excellent ironmonger whose business this was. Monsieur Pinel came out and looked at the problem. Small, dark and stocky with immensely powerful arms he reminded me at once of our blacksmith at home in Devon.

The blacksmith did an excellent job for us and has since become part of our favoured team but not before I had my own laugh at the misfortunes of others on high, slippery roofs. His apprentice, Pierre, was a gentle youngster, a pink-cheeked and tubby lad who did not immediately give the impression that he would be battling away for the honour of Lavaur rugby each weekend, rather helping his Mum with the shopping or watching a nice video tucked up snugly by the fire.

The blacksmith left the lad to clear away the chimney and returned to Lavaur. It was a sharp frosty morning and I was working near the long

'He jumped up on to the top of the chimney stack.'

ladder when I heard a crash followed by a yelp of fright. Poor Pierre had slipped on the icy roof and slithered backwards towards the edge beneath which was a long drop before the hard tarmac. The boy was clinging on to the roof for dear life, fingers and toes digging in to wherever he could get a purchase. I climbed up the ladder and offered to help him down but he was not going to budge, a look of sheer terror on his face, calling all the while for Monsieur Pinel.

I hurried indoors and telephoned the blacksmith who exploded. He cursed the lad and I could hear him giving everyone in his shop the benefit of his views on modern youth. Returning outside I was astonished to find Pierre on the ground grinning sheepishly. He pointed to the roof where I saw that a number of tiles had been removed to create a hole through which a tubby but desperate youngster had squeezed.

At this point the blacksmith returned still furious at having been called back. When he saw his lad safely on the ground and realised that the call had been a false alarm the fun really began. A verbal tirade, worthy of the best military parade grounds, assaulted the delicate ears of the poor lad. I backed slowly into the shadow of the barn well pleased that, when I had been aloft with Nick and was stumbling around, I had been able to pull rank on the old soldier and my efforts had been treated with more sympathy. Wet and icy roof tops, I decided, were places to be avoided.

The plumbing was attended to by another Lavaur worthy – Monsieur Benaben. He too came to our rescue and studied the matter, unable to comprehend the can of worms he saw confronting him once he had got amongst it all. Each joint received the same Oscar-winning performance put on for my benefit.

He would crouch down in front of whatever had been cobbled together or had ceased to function, would then push his cap to the back of his balding head, remain silent for a while and then pull slowly on his large whiskery, moustache. Eventually he would stand and turn towards me with a look of gravity on his face such as a surgeon might reserve for a sick patient for whom bad news is on the way. Before pronouncing judgement he would roll some filthy tobacco into a thin cigarette, strike up, inhale deeply then slowly shake his head.

At first he had me fooled and I was prepared for the worst – that all the plumbing had to come out this very instant, that the boiler had to be changed and that new, expensive equipment had to be installed. But then, with a mischievous grin, he would announce that just two small taps and a couple of washers had to be changed. '*C'est tout!*' Monsieur Benaben has been back on a number of occasions. The theatricals are the same each time but I have learned to brazen it out although I pretend to be impressed by the sombre gravity of it all. He has not let us down and his name and phone number are up there on the panic board.

Early in the year Rachel announced that what little money we had left was disappearing faster than it was being topped up. If the financial curve continued at this rate we would, she announced, be out of funds before the end of the summer. Somehow we had to find a way of bringing in some more cash before the clients eased the strain for us. We had a number of bookings confirmed so would not be marched off to the debtors' prison but things were looking pretty tight.

We discussed it over a tea break with Nick who, after hearing our plight, turned and said, 'Paddy, I could do with an extra pair of hands on my next job – interested?' He went on to say that he had been engaged by a young British banker who had bought an old cottage on the outskirts of a nearby village. The fellow was out in the Far East and had given Nick a broad directive to clean the place up and make it habitable.

Nick knew that I was no craftsman but he knew that I could graft with the best of them and for this he offered to pay me well. Furthermore we got along well together and, over our breaks, we used to laugh about our old army days. So, here I was – retired full Colonel off to work for a retired Lance Corporal. It was tough going and the place was quite extraordinary. The small village, a picturesque and well-known one, was just a few miles from Toulouse, the high-tech centre of southern Europe where, twenty years earlier, Concorde had been built.

But here was a house, scarcely beyond the suburbs, which barely knew civilisation. Just one cold tap in the kitchen, no bathroom, no loo in the house and not even a privvy in the garden, the place was primitive in the extreme. Upstairs just a few beds in two tatty rooms into which the rain leaked and through which the wind blew, a family of three generations had lived here like this until just a few weeks before.

And yet, along with this feudal lifestyle, went an enormous television set complete with satellite dish, and outside, in the muddy yard, two cars. I had seen only one other place like this and that was in Northern Ireland when we searched a poor area in Belfast but that was nearly thirty years before. This was 1994 and just along the road they were building space craft.

In a way it was easy as Nick had been given a free hand and set to work doing things the way he knew best. I was his labourer and together we took the place apart and put it back together again. Beams are heavy, cement is heavy and building blocks are heavy. The dust and filthy rubble stank and there was ton after ton of it, but we soldiered on and made steady progress.

Then, one day while up at the house, my world seemed to fall apart. Nick had asked me to clear out one of the small, dark back rooms. It was in a filthy state with heaps of rubble and rubbish everywhere. For an hour or so I toiled away taking barrow after barrow of rubble out to the skip until I had begun to clear a space, when I came across what I at first took to be two small boxes.

Stooping down I saw they were small home-made bird cages. I stopped quite still, horrified at the vision in my mind of the nightmare scenario. Small, wild birds would have been trapped or taken from the nest as fledglings, put in these cages and kept in this dark, damp, rat-infested back room. They would have been little song birds – goldfinches, skylarks or perhaps even nightingales taken just before the autumn migration to the far south.

The tiny birds would have been condemned to a life in these squalid little cages and I saw in my mind the dainty feet closed around the wires of the cage, the little heads pressed against the wire grill as the tiny eyes looked longingly towards the room's one small window through which the light now filtered. The heads would have been cocked as they listened to the sounds of life outside, the noises of the farmyard and the call of the wild birds still free to fly wherever they chose and to sing in the open air.

What agonies and heartaches those minute scraps of life would have suffered, kept in those ghastly conditions for the pleasure of man until they could sing no more, when their little lives would have been snuffed out and their bodies cast aside to make room for the next captives.

I exploded in rage and smashed my shovel onto those grisly relics again and again until they were nothing more than matchwood and wire. The rest of the morning I felt depressed and angry, that one black moment triggering off a feeling of despair. When we stopped for lunch Nick sensed something was amiss. 'You all right, Paddy?' he asked as we settled around the fire he had built up in the old grate.

'Oh, I don't know. Just can't get with it this morning,' I replied.

'No? Come on, what's up? You're not yourself, that's for sure.' I told him about the bird cages then went on to admit that things were pretty tough right now. We were down on cash, the pound was low and likely to get worse, bookings were none too good and the bills kept piling in. Rachel had not been too well and Tris was still struggling at school.

'Right now, Nick, I feel like packing the whole goddam thing in, eating humble pie and going back to England. Just look at what I could be doing instead of shovelling shit out here. Look at those cushy jobs I turned down – nice comfy offices, the salary rolling in each month, the pension piling up. I'm over fifty for God's sake! What the hell am I doing this for? What a bloody awful mess!'

Nick could see that this was hurting. Silent for a moment as he stirred the fire into life he turned to me. 'No,' he said quietly, 'you don't want to go back. I know you pretty well now, you know. You love it out here, really. You're just pissed off with it all now 'cos things have gone wrong. Those jobs you were on about back home, they're not for you. Honestly, all dressed up to the nines, writing speeches an' that for all them geezers. Getting your arse kicked around by that Admiral bloke. An' all that crap about poncing around London on horses with feathers in your hat. It's just not for you, Paddy. And as for all that commuting shite, forget it. You would have done your nut by now.

'Listen, you're just hacked off with it all. It's been piling up for a bit. I can see it's been tough, these things happen you know. It gets to me sometimes. I'll tell you what to do. Stop rabbiting on about what's gone wrong with it all. No lots of lolly, no smart clothes, fancy cars an' all that. Who wants it all for Christ's sake? You can't take it with you, you know. Just look at what you've got instead. You're not broke. You've got a smashing missus – she really is you know. Bosc Lebat's a fantastic pad, an' you don't owe nobody anything there. The kids are great and you've got your health. Can't be bad, can it?'

Nick was brilliant. In the simple, direct, streetwise logic of the barrack room he had put his finger on it. The remorseless pressures, the financial worries and the sheer hard physical graft had got to me and, triggered by some small, unrelated incident had momentarily brought me to my knees. But he was so right. There was everything to live for and we were far, far better off than most. But the moment had brought home just how easy it was to let things pile up and spill over. It was not the gentle, easy life in England where the retired officer could be expected to cruise gently on with his pension and some interesting little job.

Anyone contemplating making a new life for themselves in France or any other foreign country had to be prepared for hard financial times and hard physical graft if they were going to attempt anything like our plans. In addition they would have to be prepared for the occasional black moment of despair when they would wonder what on earth they were doing. Nick put on the inevitable life-saving pot of tea and later that afternoon we were to laugh about it all.

We had received a call from the owner who had asked if I would go out and buy a tractor mower and try to do something with the area outside the house. Thus, in between working for Nick and keeping our own gardens at Bosc Lebat under control, I started work in the gardens here. The mass of little sheds and fences around the old farmhouse were taken down and burned, wire, bricks and stones collected up. Rubble was cleared away, holes filled in and bushes and shrubs cut back.

A new landscape emerged and mowing began. I worked away here for as long as I could but the guest season at Bosc Lebat was not far off and I had more pressing business there. Happily my part in all this effort was over and I signed off with Nick and got on with our own preparations.

We thought that we might be able to get the large middle bedroom done before the season started so we asked Nick to come over. He reckoned his work would take about a week and, to save time, asked us to get in all the materials in advance so he could get straight on with it. He worked fast with me by his side again, doing an excellent job and leaving us to do the painting and decorating.

On these occasions I did the basic work such as undercoats, varnishing, floors and ceilings, leaving Rachel to add the colour and the feminine touch. We had cut our teeth on the other rooms so set about this, our last big room, with some confidence. And just as well too for the bookings indicated that we were going to need it and we wanted to get the job finished.

A few months later Nick came to see us and told us that he and his girlfriend were splitting up and that he had decided to leave France and to try his luck back home once more. He did not want to go back into the building trade but would like to try something in the Security line or perhaps bodyguarding.

When a young soldier in the Green Jackets, Nick had teamed up with a character known as Andy McNab. They had soldiered together for a while before going on their separate ways. Years later the Gulf

War blew up and, once the dust had settled, McNab made a fortune telling the world his story with the book *Bravo Two Zero*. Nick had since been in touch and Mcnab had offered to help – but had I any contacts?

Many years previously, while operating in Aden, I had worked with a soldier called Joe Lock. Joe, as tough as they come, had been a great soldier and a good friend but tragically, a few years after we had been serving together, he suffered a horrendous traffic accident that had left him wheelchair-bound. He fought tooth and nail to get himself up off the floor and eventually went home to Hereford where he started his own employment agency, placing ex-servicemen in all manner of jobs around the world.

I thought he might be able to use Nick so I rang him and he sounded optimistic. Nick went back to England and we heard nothing for several months. Then, one day we got a call. It was Nick calling us from a mobile phone in London. He was talking to us from the Ritz. 'It's me, Nick,' the voice whispered urgently.

'Yes, I can hear that, but what the hell's up?' I queried, imagining him to be in the middle of some ghastly marital drama.

'No, it's OK but I can't talk any louder than this. I'm doing a job in London guarding Arabs and Royalty.'

'Yes, OK, that's great, lucky old you. But why this drama over the phone, why are you whispering like that?'

'My boss and his client are just about to leave. I'm covering them, but thought I would call you up to let you know the score and to say thanks for putting me in touch with Joe. Just thought you might like to know that things have worked out, Paddy. I've got to go now. Cheers and thanks for being a pal.'

The line went dead and that was that. Few calls have given us so much pleasure. We had been sorely pressed when Nick stepped in with his fantastic offer of help and now, at long last, the favour had been returned. That night we raised our glasses to old Nick.

# CHAPTER XIV

# Life Marches On

*Shooting and the* Chasse. *Boar in the wood. Chopin and Nightingales. Wolsey Lodges.* The Times *and* Telegraph. *Lavaur – our home town. The Saturday Market.*

O ne of the great autumn events in France is the *chasse*. Here, in the rural south-west, it is as popular as anywhere and since our first days at Bosc Lebat, as we were unpacking and settling in, we used to see members of the hunt in the fields and woods around the valley. I made a mental note at the end of the last season that I would find out a little more about the great tradition.

I used to shoot in England and, during my last few years in the Army, had been chairman of a small shoot in southern England. It was a great break from the office and the ten or so guns would meet throughout the season and make a day of it. It was not a big shoot, occasionally we would might bag a hundred head of game but, more often than not, we would end the day with thirty or forty head.

Having grown up with a gun, ridden to hounds and fished the trout streams on the hills of Exmoor, I am reasonably well versed in matters such as game conservancy, the control of vermin and the way that hounds went about their business. However, as time went on, I began to feel uneasy about certain aspects of field sports. Heavily stocked game coverts that would put hundreds of birds over the guns or over-stocked rivers and lakes where the fish were just pulled from the water no longer held any appeal. As the years went by I began to question my own attitude towards killing for sport. And then one day it all came to a head.

The secretary of our shoot was meticulously fair about protocol in that nobody was given any advantage over the others, even visitors, no matter who they were. The day revolved around the draw made at the start and that was that. It was the last stand of the day and I found myself in a splendid position where a line of old trees led away from the covert that was to be beaten. Traditionally this was the best stand and so it proved today. No sooner had the beaters entered the wood than the first birds left their sanctuary and flew high along the line of oaks.

I had one of those purple patches when everything clicked. Time and again from the depths of the wood came the warning shout 'Forward!' followed by the whirr of wings and more high birds. I cannot remember how many I shot at this stand but just before the end another bird came my way and was hit fair and square, crashing to the ground a few feet in front of me. I looked at my quarry and saw a pretty little hen pheasant on her back, legs twitching before she lay still in the grass.

I stopped, looked again and suddenly felt deeply ashamed for deriving pleasure from such an act. What on earth was I thinking about, slaying a harmless and beautiful little creature such as this? She had done me no harm, and was happily taking her evening feed when she was driven into the air to be shot – by me. I hardly heard the cries of congratulations from the other guns as we gathered to check the bag and make our way back to the farm from where we had all set out in the morning. All the way home I wrestled with my conscience and have not picked up a gun for sport since.

I have found the shooting scene in France is very different – at least down here in the Tarn. The land is not keepered and there is far too much vermin about. Every village and hamlet has its own *chasse*, the boundaries carefully marked out by little signs in the hedgerows. The number of guns who will shoot over the ground is decided by the President and his deputies; in our case it is around twenty-five. Each area of the *chasse* is subdivided into smaller areas in which the hunters potter around with their dogs.

There is not much wild game at large, neither are a large number of birds released at the beginning of the season. Here, at some point during the week, usually late at night, some birds are released into the area and these are then taken by the *chasse*. The process is repeated throughout the season. A number of our guests consider this unnecessarily cruel and feel the birds should be released earlier in order to get accustomed to their wild state. I have to agree that it is not a particularly good solution but is it any better or worse than in England where the birds are fed at the same spot for weeks on end until one day, instead of being fed, they are driven into the air and over the line of waiting guns?

It is sad that there is so much ill-informed criticism of the *chasse* and the behaviour of its members. Some time during our first spring we were invited to lunch by a couple who lived near Gaillac and, while we were having lunch, the subject of the *chasse* cropped up whereupon one of the other guests heaped scorn on the whole system and condemned the hunters out of hand. 'Dreadful people,' he cried, 'Quite dreadful! The Braithwaites had all sorts of trouble with them, told them to get off their land and, the next thing they knew, the buggers had shot their cat. I wouldn't let them near our place.'

I asked him to consider what the reaction might have been in Hampshire or Norfolk if a French couple were to settle there and were to start remonstrating against the neighbouring shoot, forbidding them to come on to their land or telling the local Master of Foxhounds where to go. He thought about this and I ventured to suggest that there would be hell to pay, they would be ostracised and might well lose more than just the cat.

'That's hardly the point,' he blustered on. 'In any case these people look so ruddy awful, staggering around swathed in bandoliers, nasty cheap pump action guns, blasting away at anything that moves, their dogs quite out of control!'

He was an irritating fellow, rather aggressive, someone who is always right and who holds strong views about everyone and everything. 'Surely to goodness it doesn't matter what they look like,' I countered. 'If you really feel so strongly about the way they set about it, go and talk to the local *chasse* president. I bet you don't even know his name or where he lives. If this was England you would go along and have it out with the secretary of the hunt or shoot, wouldn't you?'

At this point our hostess, sensing that we were poles apart on this particular matter, eased the cheese dish between us and we left it like that. The fellow had missed the point completely in that those who joined the rural *chasse* were hardly men of means. They were local folk, mainly from the nearby towns and villages, who wanted to take a bit of exercise and whether or not they chose to dress up like Mexican bandits was neither here nor there.

They were delighted with what little game they bagged and which was inevitably destined for the family pot. There were no scenes at the end of the day of line upon line of birds hanging in pairs awaiting their final journey to the local wholesale butcher. Furthermore, I have yet to see any of the guns here shooting small song birds, as they were so often accused of doing.

I decided to take a closer look at our local *chasse* in case anything untoward was going on but it was very much as I thought – a harmless enough occasion. Most of them walk around slowly in pairs chatting away, their guns slung over their shoulders, clouds of dogs rushing about way out in front of them putting up anything that could move several gun lengths out of any danger.

Odd Job is one of the stalwarts of our *chasse* and on Sundays he and his chums will call the midday halt and gather around in a barn just down the road where they will tuck into an enormous picnic washed down with bottles of local wine. If we pass them in the car or on our walk we always draw smiles, waves and raised glasses.

The one point of conflict with our *chasse* is that we did not like the idea of the wildlife on our land being disturbed too often. From time to time some of the *chasse* would walk through our wood and I checked this out with Odd Job, explaining that we had no quarrel at all with the *chasse* but would they, if possible, keep out of the wood where we want the wildlife to go undisturbed. I explained also that I would do what I could to keep down the vermin that was so much in evidence.

'*Oui*, Monsieur King, I will see what can be done. But you know that, by law, they are allowed onto your land although they must not discharge their guns within one hundred and fifty metres of the house. Did you know that?' I replied that we did, however we would like him to see what might be arranged. The *chasse* now leaves us in peace and except for one particular occasion have given us a wide berth. I shudder to think how they would have all reacted had I started jumping up and down, shouting at them and creating a scene.

The one time that all caution was thrown to the winds was when a small group of wild boar were spotted in our big wood. Not even a minefield would have stopped the *chasse* and their followers. The wood was surrounded and a couple of old sweats entered from the top end with their dogs. Almost at once a deep baying broke out as the hounds got on to their quarry. Before long two young *sangliers* broke cover and made a break for it only to be felled by the cordon. The third, an old tusker, was more wary and gave the dogs and handlers a run for their money in the wood before he too chanced his luck and was despatched.

Great celebrations followed, including a special *chasse* supper in the village to which we were invited. Sadly we were unable to attend but a small deputation came to see us the following day bearing a large haunch of *sanglier* which we kept for a while before Rachel produced a feast – our own boar, cooked with our own apples and walnuts, spiced with our own herbs and marinated in the deep red wine of the Tarn. All of this followed by fresh local cheeses washed down with a few bottles of the best Gaillac wine, was a meal to remember.

Time had moved on. Rachel and I had been struggling with various projects and had scarcely noticed how the long months of winter had passed. Spring comes early to the Tarn and the local farmers tell us that once February has been and gone winter is all but over. It is not far from the truth and by now, early April, the evenings were drawing out and the sun was rising ever higher in the sky.

Finally, after many weeks of painstaking work, Monsieur Parisot brought the piano back and we set it up in its new home next to the dining room. Initially it went out of tune quite frequently and we saw much of him as he returned time and again to fine tune the notes or to ease the movements within the great instrument. This, so he told us, was quite usual when so much had been done but gradually the full movement returned and Rachel began to play once more.

My mother had been a pianist in her youth and when I was young she used to play in the evenings with the drawing-room windows open. Outside I could always hear birds singing. Those, she would explain, are nightingales and they are singing back to the piano. I was enchanted at the sound but as I grew older I dismissed the story as pure fantasy.

Here in south-west France we are blessed with wonderful bird life including a huge influx of summer visitors many of them small songbirds such as warblers and nightingales. Now here they really were singing back to Rachel as she played in the evenings with the music-room windows open. Of all that she plays, Chopin is my favourite and sometimes, when we are alone, I will sit on the bench by the open window as she plays a selection of Nocturnes and will listen spellbound as these marvellous little birds reply to her music with their beautiful deep, warbling song.

Gradually we got the feeling that we were getting on top of things and that the very worst of the tasks were now behind us. It had indeed been a bit of a gallop and we accepted the ups and downs we had experienced as no more than a part of life. However the one thing we will not accept is that we, or anyone else who has come out to France, have been lucky to have done what we have. Sometimes a guest will tell us that they were thinking of doing just this but there were some problems at home which put them off – how lucky we were to be able to make the break.

There will always be problems at home, always many good reasons why such a venture is not possible at the time – the childrens' education, the children after their education, elderly parents or whatever. Those folk will never do it. They are the daydreamers and romancers who will always find some convenient excuse to put it off. If it is going to be done then it has to be prepared carefully and the plunge taken. It's no good hovering around up there on the diving board, knees knocking together, staring down into the water.

Our second season was approaching and bookings, while we still had plenty of room to spare, had gone well with a sudden rush in the early spring. Right from the outset we had decided to find a niche at the top end of the market. Tracking down those we considered to be the sort of clients we wanted at Bosc Lebat was another matter entirely and had to be orchestrated carefully.

I began by writing an article in my school magazine and placing an advertisement in the *Pennant* – the magazine of the armed forces Officers' Pension Society. Relatives and friends helped spread the word but I was looking for some organisation that dealt with what we were trying to achieve.

A number of friends had mentioned an English-based company called Wolsey Lodges. For several years they had been dealing with just our type of home throughout the UK and now, so we were told, they had widened their membership and started to include homes on the continent. We were encouraged to contact them and see if there might be a meeting of the waters.

They proved to be exactly what we were after. In brief, it is a consortium of privately owned homes who open their doors to guests. The organisation is named after King Henry VIII's famous Lord Chancellor – Cardinal Wolsey – who toured the realm expecting generous hospitality from suitable country houses along the way. Staying at a Wolsey Lodge is something of a social experience as it is a private home and not a hotel. Thus the relationship between hosts and guests, indeed between the guests themselves, is more akin to a house party than found in the standard B&B residence.

Wolsey Lodges now has some 200 members throughout the UK and a dozen or so in the rest of Europe. They produce a beautifully presented brochure and explain their philosophy in some detail to all those who might wish to stay at one of the establishments. The Dos and Don'ts for the guests make interesting and amusing reading. Among other things you are advised that the idea of placing your shoes outside the bedroom door to be cleaned is likely to be a fruitless exercise, and that feeding the baby at the dinner table will not win many bouquets for tact or diplomacy.

Initially, it appears that the cards are stacked heavily in favour of the homeowners, in that guests will arrive, bound to a set of strict rules, having to tread warily, fearful of upsetting their prickly and uncompromising hosts. This is by no means the case.

Having studied the idea for a while we wrote off and, after filling in a number of questionnaires, were told that we would be visited. During the visit we, our home and the way we intended to set about our business, would be considered by the visitors. In short we were in for a good old-fashioned inspection from top to toe.

By the time they came to see us our season was up and running but we found a quiet spell in between bookings and planned the visit accordingly. We had decided to be quite open with them explaining that this was a new experience for us and that we would not make any special effort on their behalf. This, so we thought, would be hopelessly transparent and, in any case, we had no idea what sort of performance to lay on.

The visit was made by the chairman of the company who came with his wife, the company secretary. While we knew that we were on parade, it was a very relaxed affair and our guests went out of their way to put our minds at ease. After dinner Rachel played for a while and early next morning they went for a walk and swam in the pool before going on their way. A short while after they left we had a phone call – it was our guests inviting us to become members.

Wolsey Lodges suggests the prices that we, their members, should ask and any alterations are cleared with them. Should somebody, for any reason, wish to raise their prices unduly, they are told that they can indeed but that they would have to leave the consortium. This is a good idea in that it prevents anyone from using the company name in order to make undue profit. Membership is renewed annually and the members are advised that clients are encouraged to raise any issues with the company if they are unhappy with the way things have gone. Should this occur Wolsey Lodges would discuss the complaint with the member concerned and, if things continued in this fashion, something would have to be done.

While in no way over-controlled, members of Wolsey Lodges go about their business within clear guidelines, all of which keeps us on our toes and the standards of the whole consortium up to the mark. In this way both guests and hosts are asked to think about each other. It is a very clever formula that has brought us a considerable number of guests, many of whom have since become friends. The good name of the company is now becoming well known internationally and we have enjoyed visits from all over the world.

Wolsey Lodges was a major breakthrough and all that remained now was to somehow get some good publicity. Here again we were in luck. An old friend of ours rang and asked if we were interested in getting some free publicity from *The Times* newspaper. She went on to explain that she had received a call from a journalist friend in London who had discussed the subject of the British in France at some length. A year previously one of the TV channels had run a series in which a catalogue of disasters in France had portrayed the British in a very poor light. There were stories of people going bankrupt, of others falling foul of the system, marriages breaking up and so on – all most unfortunate publicity.

The journalist wanted to get things into perspective. Surely, she thought, there must be some successful stories where businesses were up and running, and where people were happy with their lot. Our name had been put forward and we were scheduled to go on the short list.

Eventually we heard from the great newspaper. The short brief I had written won us a place and finally, many months later, we and three others had a page of the travel section devoted to our adventures. A few years later we had a similar stroke of luck and appeared in the Travel Section of the *Weekend Telegraph*. Suzanne Lowry, then writing for the paper, had been given our name and came over with a photographer to do the article. We learned later that she lived close by on the edge of the Black Mountains and we have now become good friends.

We realise now just how valuable such promotion is to a tiny business struggling along. Advertising is crucial to our survival. It is expensive and time-consuming but is something we have to consider carefully if we want to attract the sort of clients we are seeking.

We had not fully appreciated quite how important it was to be situated close to a town until a number of guests had been to stay with us. We had decided that, for our own purposes, it was essential but had not realised that the guests needed such a place as well. Lavaur, like every other town in France, boasts its wide, tree-lined boulevards where old men gather to pass the time or conduct their daily game of boules. Around the Centre Ville there are numerous small cafes with tables set out in the sun where our guests invariably spend an hour or two watching the world go by. Once on holiday they want to relax and enjoy a cup of coffee or glass of wine, absorbing the local scene, while dashing off the inevitable postcards.

The Saturday market in Lavaur is the occasion of the week and something not to be missed. Either Rachel or I go in early to our favourite stalls to buy olives, fresh cheeses or sliced meat which we offer to our guests with their aperitifs in the evening before they go out to dinner. The great olive stall alone is worth a visit and there are always around thirty or so different varieties on display in large tubs. The olive man is a keen rugby fan and we always chat about the Five Nations, the

*'The Saturday market in Lavaur is the occasion of the week.'*

fortunes of the local clubs or how professionalism has changed the game.

Next to them there are delicious dried fruits, spices and nuts laid out for inspection. Beyond them our cheese lady has her small stall with appetizing homemade sheep and goat cheeses laid out temptingly. Lines of stalls are laden with an enormous variety of local produce all beautifully arranged to catch the eye of the morning crowds. Huge dishes of gently cooking paella and poultry turning slowly on the spit tempt those with an early appetite as do the stalls full of mouth-watering cakes and pastries.

The vendors work hard for their living, usually rising well before dawn. They are cheerful, boisterous, fiercely independent and woe betide any petty official who comes along to remonstrate with them about food hygiene or other nonsensical regulations, especially if the directive comes from Brussels. All the meats are cut with the same knife which is then wiped as clean as the rather dubious apron permits. Cheeses are cut into portions with the same slice.

The wares, all fully exposed to the elements, are picked up and examined closely by the farmers and their wives who have just been handling livestock or loading poultry into the back of the car. The whole affair is treated in the same open, carefree manner that has been the case for ever and a day.

No one suffers any ill effects from this: there is no food poisoning, no salmonella and no outbreak of this or that, in fact no need at all for any interference from the EEC and their health and safety officials. And this is where the rural French come into their own. If Brussels attempts to impose any such restrictions on these country folk, unless they see the good sense in it, the matter is simply ignored, treated with contempt and life carries on uninterrupted.

A few years back one such official did appear in the Gers. He made the grave mistake of threatening the vendors with legal action if they failed to comply with the new standards. The fellow was surrounded by an angry crowd, roughed up and sent on his way. Nobody here wants that sort of change, nobody has asked for change and nobody can see any reason it. Life, in this corner of France, goes quietly on its way just as it has always done and just as it should.

# CHAPTER XV

# The Circle Gets Ever Wider

*French neighbours. Expatriot social life. The British in the Tarn.*
*The International community.*

Our diaries, Christmas letters and visitors' books for the first two or three years bring countless memories flooding back. Those early, busy days enabled us to put down our roots, but time has moved on and, as I write this, incredible though it may seem, we have just completed our seventh season at Bosc Lebat. It is never too late to learn about the business and even now we are constantly being surprised by this or that or some sudden new event that causes the adrenaline to surge.

The early years were so hectic and life passed so quickly that we had little time to do anything other than react to the immediate. Gradually the pace slackened, however, and we began to look around. At last there was time to meet new people, to get out and explore the surrounding countryside, as well as continuing with the development of the business. Our tale would not be complete without a brief glance back over this period to bring our story up to date.

We see Jonathan, our American neighbour, and his family frequently and, now that Rachel has started to teach again, Julian, their younger son, cycles up for lessons. Alex, the older boy and a big, strong lad who followed Tristan into Lavaur rugby, comes and helps me in the woods when I need an extra pair of hands. There are just four other houses in our valley, one of which we pass each day on our walk.

184

Les Targettes is home to a trio of simple country folk. Monsieur Carvet, now over seventy, lives here with his sister and mother. She, a quite remarkable old lady, well over ninety, is still with us in every sense and gets out there with the pitchfork when her neighbour, Monsieur Martin the farmer, cuts the hay along the edges of the road.

They keep themselves to themselves, draw their water from the well in the garden, tend their chickens and spend hours every day in their vegetable garden which is ploughed for them each spring by a kindly neighbouring farmer. In his youth Monsieur Carvet used to work at Bosc Lebat and has many tales to tell of life in the valley before the War.

We see them often and, when time permits, stop for a chat. The south-west accent has a deep rolling burr, the word is spoken quickly and the whole business becomes further complicated when the older countryfolk slip back into the dialect of Occitane. Tristan claims to be able to understand them as does Rachel from time to time, but I am quite beaten by it all. Once confronted by the challenge, I search desperately for clues from the waving arms, gesticulations and any other signals that might let me in on the secret. I would dearly love to talk to the older farmers and countryfolk about life here in the valley many years ago.

One day last winter Rachel was walking the dogs past their house when Patch disappeared into a deep drain under the road. Suddenly a fearful commotion erupted right under the spot where she was standing. Not the excited yap of a terrier marking some quarry, rather a full-blooded dog fight. No quarter was being given and no prisoners were going to be taken.

Try as she might she could not get him away. Once he dragged his opponent to the mouth of the drain only to be dragged back in again, snarling viciously, locked in combat. Seeing a large pool of dark, red blood where they had just been Rachel took fright and ran to the Carvets for help. The gallant trio appeared with brooms and shovels ready to do battle for Patch but he was not going to let go – not even to orders in Occitane.

Now, thoroughly alarmed and, urged on by her supporters to do something about it quickly, Rachel called me. After some time I managed to haul him away from whatever it was down there and it was obvious that there had been a battle royal. Patch, though not badly wounded, had a number of small wounds beneath the mass of blood covering his head, chest and legs. To any good Jack Russell this was of no consequence and he trotted home with me, tail in the air, to be cleaned up and have his wounds dressed.

Next morning Monsieur Carvet called us and enquired anxiously about Patch. He is fine we replied. Thank you for your call but why the concern? Monsieur Carvet explained that on inspecting the battleground he had come across a big dog fox, stone dead, head half removed. Patch had shown courage beyond the call of duty and had stood defiantly between the villain and Monsieur Carvet's flock of free-range chickens. Parson Jack Russell himself would have been proud of his protégé, and our hero, if little fox terriers were able to walk tall, would have been doing just that.

Sometime later the Carvets had trouble with their phone and asked us to call France Telecom. Next time I passed the house Monsieur tried to press ten Francs into my hand for my efforts. Thoroughly embarrassed by this gesture I would not entertain the idea. I told him that he should not consider such a thing and that, before long, it would be me asking him for help. Early the following morning there was a knock on the kitchen door and Monsieur Carvet had come to see us again. Spruced up in his walking-out best, hair brushed flat and reeking of some impossible aftershave, he had walked up to Bosc Lebat and, in a touching little gesture, brought us a basket of fresh eggs for our trouble.

Beyond the Carvets is the lovely old farm where Monsieur Martin lives with his family. He farms much of the land in the valley and I had known him since the infamous occasion I had gone and attempted to beg a trailerload of old manure for my new roses. He runs a large herd of mixed beef and dairy cattle that sometimes graze the open pastures in the valley. The lovely, gentle beasts are always tended by a cowherd, sometimes it was his old father, sometimes another member of the family, but more often than not it is his good wife.

Madame Martin is a fine figure and we are left in little doubt as to the driving force in La Rendie – their homestead. Back ramrod straight, bearded chin thrust forward and her cattle stick thrust behind her back between her arms, she stands guard, nothing escaping her gaze. As I pass by she looks directly at me, her beady eyes twinkling brightly, checking my turnout and the pace of my step. Even now my pulse quickens as though I am on parade at Sandhurst under the forbidding gaze of the Sergeant Major whose attention I used to dread so. A redoubtable lady indeed and in the early days I used to approach her with some trepidation, my cheery greeting ready the instant she turned my way.

I know her better now and, beneath the stern gaze, there is a warm, homely character, one who always has a smile and a wave as we pass by. I have found her stall at the poultry market and on Saturdays I watch from some distance as, friends gathered around, she passes on the news and gossip from Massac, including no doubt anything of interest from Bosc Lebat.

He, poor chap, had a terrible tractor accident when the machine rolled in a field and badly crushed him. He lay there for several hours before help came and for months was away in hospital, the farm left to Madame Martin. She coped magnificently, helped by the large family and neighbours rallying to support the stricken homestead. Happily he is now back with us but, badly crippled, he has taken to driving everywhere in an ancient, smoking and battered Renault that coughs and splutters on its rounds. By his side sits Madame, head erect, jaw square and eyes to the front.

They stopped by the house the other day while I was in the orchard. Smoke pouring from his old car Monsieur Martin staggered out, opened up the bonnet and waved away what fumes he could with his large and ancient straw hat while peering into the bowels of the old car. I hurried across and asked him what he thought the matter was. 'Dunno,' he quipped. 'If 'twas a horse I could tell you, but not this thing.' Slamming the bonnet shut, he kicked the wheel hard and climbed back in before grinding off up the hill, smoke still pouring forth, Madame's eyes firmly on the road ahead.

And on our other side is Jacques' sheep farm. He has sold it now as it was all getting too much for his dear old mother who looked after him, doing the housework and gardening as well. Jacques was sixty and had had enough so they put the place on the market and found a buyer. No sooner had they gone than we received an invitation to a great family celebration – the old lady had just been presented with her first great-great-grandchild. The huge family were being assembled from far and wide and they had been kind enough to ask us to join them.

It was a grand occasion held in the corn yard of one of their big family farms nearby, with supper in one of the barns. A field behind the farmhouse had been turned into a camping site to cater for the family who had been summoned from all over France. Fairy lights were strung beneath the trees in front of the house, accordion music played softly in the background and we watched fascinated as the family met in the great yard where some, not having seen each other for years, were quite overcome with emotion. Behind them all two sheep were slowly turning on the spit. Swarms of barefoot grandchildren and great-grandchildren were dashing about whilst the womenfolk bustled to and fro preparing the meal.

Like many social occasions here it began slowly and we wondered if it would ever get off the ground. It did, and gradually the pace quickened as the young were collected together and sent on their rounds with trays of delicious food and jugs of aperitif. The old lady had been a settler in Morocco where she and her husband had brought up their ten children until the troubles flared into open rebellion and President de Gaulle ordered their rescue.

The Gaudeberts and many others we know had been here since then, farming the land in the hills around us. Now the clan had gathered.

Eight of the surviving children, twenty-three grandchildren and countless youngsters plus the one tiny addition made up the party with just ourselves plus a few close French friends and neighbours.

More than ninety of us sat down in the barn to eat, beginning with yet more mouth-watering starters a l'Afrique du Nord, washed down with great jugs of wine. The first sheep, garnished with garlic and rosemary, together with all its attendant trimmings and vegetables was almost enough for us but huge platters of mutton kept on doing the rounds. Jackets and ties were off, and, come midnight Rachel and I were eating and drinking for England.

Then after the meal the singing began. Deep, slow, emotional songs of the settlers rang out through the night, the family gathered around in a huge throng while the old matriarch sat at the head of the table. From time to time she would take up a small child in her arms, on others she would quietly dab a tear from her eyes as some poignant song brought memories of younger days flooding back. What an occasion and how honoured we were to be asked to celebrate the great event!

I mentioned earlier that there were not many other British folk around Lavaur. Jerry Baker and his entourage with all their goings on had made up for most of that but in our early days we were more or less on our own. Recently others have come to live close by but, by and large, Lavaur is not regarded as the place to be. A little further north there is a triangle of towns – Gaillac, the centre of the local wine industry, Albi, the historic cathedral city, and Cordes, a famous hilltop bastide town. Here, in what has become known as the Golden Triangle, the British community have chosen to settle in considerable numbers. After a time we began to meet some of them and, as the years went by, we came to see and learn more about life amidst the expatriot community.

I have known such communities all my life, and have a fair understanding of the advantages and the attendant problems for people living close together in a foreign land. I had seen the European cantonments in British Guiana, the mining and engineering com-

'Then after the meal the singing began.'

munities in Arabia, the British communities in the Far East and had my own experiences of such life on military estates in both the UK and overseas.

It was natural for people to congregate, especially in a foreign country, but I learned to develop a certain wariness of being caught up in such an environment in which people lived so close to each other. Sometimes life would become claustrophobic and a feeling of frustration would develop as people sought to escape the attention of others or who simply wanted a bit of privacy. We both preferred to be a little way back from such a situation – a bit more on our own.

Life in a small community, or indeed a small community within a larger community such as the British here in France, is not always easy. Living together produces a close-knit community, very often harmonious and mutually supportive but, on occasions when disagreements arise or something goes amiss, as surely they will, it can become difficult for everybody concerned. There is nowhere to hide and everybody seems to know what is going on: or likes to think they do.

This is not to suggest that the Bosc Lebat household kept their heads down and tucked themselves away from the world. Far from it, we have made a huge number of friends around the Tarn and elsewhere but are content to be just that step back from becoming inextricably tangled up in it all. I well remember one occasion, early on. We had been invited to a house party and, very much the newcomers, were aware that eyes were cast in our direction.

I was standing on my own, cautiously eyeing those around me, when a rather overpowering lady swooped down on me and, exhaling a cloud of smoke, peered closely at me and said, 'Hello, you're new here, aren't you?' I replied that we had not been here very long, to which I received the somewhat incongruous reply, 'Well, don't worry about it, everyone but everyone here's so frightfully nice.' With that, and her curiosity no doubt satisfied, she eased herself past me and away into the crowd.

She was followed some moments later by a heavily built man who sauntered across to check out the new arrivals. 'Hullo, young man,' he boomed, 'I know who you are. From Lavaur aren't you? That fellow Baker still there? Don't go near the bloke, he's up to no good, I'm warning you.' I had met Jerry a few weeks previously and already I had formed my own opinion of him.

These few moments apart, everybody we met made us fell welcome and offered us good advice on life in France. The fact that we did not get to know many people for some time was simply because we were working flat out at Bosc Lebat rather than anything to do with geography or personalities. The more we got to know our neighbours the more we came to realise that we had come to live amongst a group of diverse and interesting people, nearly all of whom have an adventure of their own to tell.

People have come to live here from all walks of life and backgrounds, all sorts of professions and in all manner of circumstances. Most have arrived without a great deal of money and have had something of a struggle to get the new life up and away. Many, like us, have had to make ends meet by doing something that would bring in additional income. Others have arrived with young children who have gone into the French education system, while yet others are fully retired.

Some, like Rachel and myself, have found themselves at something of a crossroads and want to make a go of their new life together in a totally different environment. However, amid all this diversity, there is one common strand which links everyone together. Everyone has made the great decision to make the move and have got on with it. There is something of the pioneer spirit about and we soon found that the great majority of folk who have come here are strong, positive characters.

Several of those we met set out with an idea similar to our own and have gone into the holiday business. The amount of work that has been done is simply staggering and we have been inside some beautiful homes with pretty *gîtes* and lovely pools, none of which came easily. Great effort has been made to modernise and restore old farms and cottages in keeping with the style of architecture and the surrounding countryside.

Others have gone into the world of property and become *immobiliers* whilst others still have tried their hand at producing wine.

The few brave souls who became *vignerons* have my greatest admiration for taking on the French at their own game. The world is overflowing with wine and the business is now fraught with never-ending lists of rules, regulations and mountains of paperwork. But there are a few, I am proud to say, who have won through and amongst the wines of Gaillac some of the most popular have been produced by British growers. We always delight in serving them to our French friends when they come to dinner and watch with some satisfaction when they nod their heads in approval and reach for the bottle to study the label.

There are a few we have come across who, in spite of their best efforts, have found life all too difficult. They lead something of a hand-to-mouth existence, unable to make progress but are unwilling or unable to face life again in Britain. They are in a dilemma and we worry for them. An adventure such as this has to be thought through with the greatest of care. The climate might be better, the lifestyle might sound more fun, but it does not come free and people need a bit more than just enough for a glass of wine and a baguette or two.

At the other end of the scale are a few immensely wealthy families who have come here for the good life, can afford to live that way and flit backwards and forwards to their other homes, business interests and other ways of life. Most have played it right, realising that the community amongst whom they have come to live chose to escape the rat race and are none too impressed by the trappings of great wealth.

One couple, living some way to our south, played their cards quite differently, the lady of the house outrageously flaunting her husband's money. It has been fascinating watching the reactions and listening to the comments of those who have been affected by this behaviour, some of whom allowed their emotions to get into a muddle. One or two fawned upon the newcomers, ingratiating themselves, all the while grinding their teeth in angst while others tried to turn their backs only to turn round again hurriedly in order to accept the dinner invitation.

I was reminded immediately of the time when a very senior general came to take up command. His wife, revelling in his position, constantly and cruelly scored cheap points off those who neither wished to nor were able to compete. Money, today, is power and usually goes to the heads of those in which there is little else. Rank, position or wealth handled discreetly and with dignity is attractive, indeed seductive; but those who cannot do so or who know no better eventually reveal the true nature of their character.

Fairly soon after the piano had been reinstated and Rachel had begun to play again, we had a call from some friends beyond Gaillac. A small group had clubbed together in order to raise money for a particular French charity. Among the money-raising activities there was to be a dinner in Cordes and the caller wanted to know if Rachel would consider playing. Any pianist worth his or her salt needs to practice for at least two or three hours a day and, if performances are to be given, this needs to be doubled. For certain the hands of the pianist should not be heavily involved in washing, scrubbing, painting, sewing, cooking and so forth.

Rachel took a deep breath, agreed to the request and put on a short programme of Haydn and Chopin in front of the hundred or so diners. She claimed to have played dreadfully but the applause was sincere and, as a result of this, she began to meet other musicians. We know several now and from time to time they meet here and an evening of chamber music is arranged.

I knew little about the world of music before we met and had no idea that the great composers would often write short pieces for their friends, while social occasions would be arranged around playing or singing in each other's houses. How magic it must have been to have had the young Mozart or Schubert living nearby who, when invited over to dinner, would have come to the door, not with a box of chocolates or bunch of flowers for the hostess, but with a piece of music dedicated to her instead. Once dinner was over this handwritten draft would have had its world premier.

194

It was not long before the Lavaur Choral Society found Rachel and managed to persuade her to accompany them through the long winter months of preparation for the summer concerts. Towards the end of last year they asked if they could hold their annual end-of-season dinner at Bosc Lebat after they had finished their programme of music. Thankfully a catering firm came along and took the place over for the evening when around seventy-five of us sat down to supper under the trees in the front garden.

After supper the singing began, accompanied by Rachel from inside the house with Michel, their director, conducting from the music-room window. The choir sat in a large semi-circle around him and sang some of the pieces they had performed during the summer, concluding with Mozart's evocative 'Laudate Dominum'. It was a lovely, still evening but rather too hot and sultry. The party went on until some time after midnight when thunder rumbled ominously in the distance causing the caterers to emerge from the shadows and sweep everything hastily away before the heavens opened.

In recent years the Tarn has been found by the wider international community and, in addition to our British and French friends, we can count Danes, Norwegians, Swedes, Germans, Poles, Russians and Americans. Most are in a similar position to us in that they have fallen in love with this part of France and have decided to make a new life here. In many cases they, too, have had something of a struggle to get the homes modernised and comfortable. The community is full of characters and many have tales of their own to tell.

Klaus, a German neighbour, lives with his Russian wife Anita in a splendid chateau a few miles to our east. He is a cheerful cove and they both love to entertain. Involved in numerous business ventures near St Petersburg he sometimes flies in his business associates from Russia to stay in the chateau. They are a pretty serious, humourless bunch who, dressed in their shiny suits and hidden behind the darkest of glasses, prefer to remain in the shadows.

They rarely acknowledge my efforts to communicate and share little of Klaus's bonhomie. I have heard tales of such characters and, having got their message that small talk is not much fun, I give them a wide berth. Later and when we are alone I try to get Klaus to tell me something about his business activities in far off Petrokrepost. Quick on his feet, he laughs, evading my questions cleverly, failing to recall anything of significance and suggesting that we turn our attention to a glass or two of chilled wine instead.

Roman Komorovski, our good Polish friend, tells awesome stories of his family's flight from their ancestral home in Poland at the outset of the last war. They arrived in the West with little more than they could carry, having lost everything to either the Russian or German invaders. His stories make our own simple efforts of cruising sedately down the autoroutes to our new life seem rather pathetic in comparison. He is heavily engaged in restoring a beautiful old farmhouse near the little market town of Lisle sur Tarn, doing almost all of the work in the house and gardens himself.

Another whose company we greatly enjoy is Bertel Ohlsen from Denmark. For many years he was one of Denmark's leading cellists before an accident to his hand curtailed his playing career. He has come to live in a lovely stone farmhouse set amidst the vines high in the hills above Gaillac, bringing with him his immense knowledge of music and his beautiful rich bass voice.

He lives there alone and is restoring the house and outbuildings bit by bit. Bertel, known to us as The Great Dane on account of his physique, has become a very close friend, he and Rachel often teaming up and entertaining our guests with a programme of songs and music. Martha and Tim Brosnahan, some American friends, live near Carcassonne. They have set up their own successful holiday business, running a number of self-contained apartments in a wing of their house which lies surrounded by the vines of Corbieres and looks out on to the Pyrenees. These and many others enrich our lives with their company.

Gradually we have come to feel as if we are now moving within a number of widely differing circles of friends and acquaintances. We have been introduced to a number of French friends, we have got to know a considerable number of international folk, there are our British friends and, finally, Rachel's widening circle of musical contacts.

## CHAPTER XVI

# *And Finally – What Now?*

*Visitors from further afield and yet more fast balls! A little local
history. Towards the end of the day – and what now?*

We ask those who are going to stay in the *gîte* to reach Bosc Lebat
sometime late in the afternoon when we have had time to
prepare the place for them. Once they have settled I go across and
explain how our system works, after which we leave them alone to get
on with their holiday. The only social activity we arrange is for them to
join us for aperitifs early in their stay so we can get to know each other
and they can meet any house guests that are about. It is a simple touch,
something we learned from one of the other British families which,
inevitably, helps to break the ice.

Patch and Alice are quick to note if there are children around, their
presence usually signalling barbeques, walks, games and other important
events. The very last part of my daily routine is to walk the dogs around
the houses just before we turn in. In the summer we often come across
the party who have taken the *gîte*, sitting quietly in their garden with a
glass of wine after a barbeque, listening to the crickets and waiting to
catch a glimpse of the barn owls.

We have had some fascinating people to stay in the *gîte*, and many
have returned for a second or third time. One day a caller from Holland
asked if there was a piano in the vicinity. Rachel replied cautiously that
there was, to which came the next question as to whether or not it was a
good one. Now, prepared for anything, she replied that it was indeed a

very good one and asked why. It transpired that the son of this Jewish family was preparing himself for the entrance exams to the Tel Aviv conservatoire and needed to practise for several hours a day. Realising immediately that the boy's music must be of the highest quality she offered him the use of her piano.

Theo was a very talented young pianist and played for five or six hours a day throughout their stay here. He was principally a jazz pianist and, although just eighteen, played Gershwin's Rhapsody in Blue without a note of music in front of him. However he had to prepare some classical pieces as well and here Rachel was able to give him some assistance. Later we learned with delight that he had been accepted and, even as I write, we are awaiting the family's return for another holiday.

Another musician who came with his young family was of Jewish extraction also. Walter's family had fled to this part of France from his native Germany before the War and took up residence in the country where, for many years, he practised as a pediatrician. Now retired, he is free to indulge in his great love of the cello and plays with chamber groups in Paris.

He came to stay with his daughter and three little grandchildren having met Rachel at a music festival in Venice. They often played together and on the last evening played until late as Valerie and I sat listening to them. I looked across at his daughter and saw that she was crying silently. Seeing my look of concern through her tears, she laughed and said, 'Don't worry, there is nothing wrong. It's just that I have never heard Papa playing so beautifully before.' The music was indeed wonderful.

Some years ago we had a delightful Canadian couple staying in the *gîte* for the winter. Alan was working on one of the space projects in Toulouse and he and his wife, Judy, had taken the place until late spring. We saw lots of them and often had meals or drinks together. They used to ask friends over from America where Alan was based and one day an enormous Texan – John – arrived for a week. We managed to extend the spare bed upstairs to accommodate his great frame and he seemed happy enough with life.

Just before his arrival a French family came and asked us if their daughter and son-in-law could spend their wedding night here at Bosc Lebat. We advised the young couple to come and make sure they knew where we were and to check the layout of Bosc Lebat, as French weddings tend to go on until the small hours when they would have to find their own way around. The great day came and, as no recce party had called, we left the lights on, doors unlocked and retired for the night expecting the dogs to warn us of their arrival. As dawn was breaking I heard a car but nobody appeared and I began to think it was a false alarm.

A short while later, hearing footsteps, I pulled on my dressing gown and went out to greet the newly weds. Around the corner came the beautiful young bride, bouquet in one hand, a large bottle of champagne in the other whilst, a dutiful pace behind her, came her man carrying the suitcases. Unused to welcoming bridal couples at my front door, let alone in my night clothes, I took them straight up to their room where I was advised that they would not be down early next morning. I beat a tactful retreat, however only a few hours later we were surprised to see them down for breakfast at the usual hour and listened fascinated as they told us how they found their way to our front door.

Big John, our Texan visitor, was a confirmed bachelor and for some years Alan and Judy had been pulling his leg about his matrimonial situation. They threatened to get him married off at whatever the cost, by fair means or foul, even offering to find him a bride. Like so many very big men he was shy and somewhat sensitive to such banter and after a while he became deeply suspicious when strange females appeared in the Kidds' house, believing they had been produced for his benefit.

Our bridal couple had indeed arrived as planned but, instead of coming to our door, went instead to the *gîte* where they found the front door open and as nobody was about tiptoed in silently and made their way upstairs to the first bedroom – just as they had been instructed to do in Bosc Lebat. Opening the door to what she thought would be the bridal chamber the young bride saw, stretched out on the bed, this huge giant of a man, 6' 6" tall and nearly 18 stones, fast asleep and dead to the world!

We told them about his deep suspicion of the Kidds' matchmaking plans and tried to imagine who might have done what to whom had the poor chap woken up and seen what was looking down at him in the dawn light. Later when we told John the story, the great fellow blushed deep crimson and, after a few moments thought said, 'If I had awoken I would 'a thought I had a' died and gone to heaven!'

Shortly after this we had another bridal couple here on their wedding night. Our doctor's daughter was to be married in Lavaur but this was a far more organised affair. As soon as they heard about the presence of Big John and the various permutations for front doors, stairways and bedrooms, we were subjected to a full-blown recce well in advance to spy out the land and take careful note of what lay where.

House guests start arriving around Easter although we have had parties here for the New Year. On these occasions we either go out to one of our favourite restaurants or ask them to include evening dress in their luggage and make a party of it back here. The same as for the *gîte*, we ask our house guests to arrive in time for tea and make a point of inviting them to have dinner with us on their first evening here. They will have had a long journey and, once settled, the thought of having to turn round and go off in search of a restaurant, is not treated with much enthusiasm. Thereafter we suggest that they do take themselves off and try some of our local restaurants or taverns.

We are fortunate here in that there are many quite excellent places to eat, all reasonably priced and within a short drive. Toulouse is just over half an hour away for those who wish to seek out the very highest standards of cuisine and where there is every conceivable choice of menu. But for us, some of the local haunts are as good as any, many offering extensive wine lists with the meal.

We leave our guests to come and go as they please. Occasionally we have people who have come down this way to look at property. As we have been through the whole thing from A-Z this is always an interesting exercise. While not pretending to be experts, we have learned a great deal over the years – some of it the hard way – and are more than happy to talk through any ideas they might have. Some pick our brains, others arrive, their minds already made up on what they want and how much they think it is all going to cost.

Nothing we suggest will change their minds yet sometimes their ideas are screaming out for advice or caution. I work with a local agent and, once I know what people are looking for, I put them in touch and they are shown a number of possibilities. Then, of course, the questions start coming thick and fast.

Entertaining our guests as we do is fun and we derive great pleasure from sitting and chatting to them over a glass of wine. Most come from the UK but more are now coming from further afield, many from America some from South Africa. One particular couple who came back for a second visit last year were our first billionaires.

Alan and Lorraine White come from California but both were born in England. Alan began life as a humble Lincolnshire farm boy before emigrating to America at the age of eighteen to seek fame and fortune across the Atlantic. The Vietnam War was in full swing at the time and young Alan had his collar fingered by Uncle Sam who told him either to take himself off home or to join the US Forces.

He chose the latter option, joined the US Marines and saw action in Khee Sahn. While doing his bit he met up with a number of characters who shared his fascination for the early computers with which they were being asked to do much of their work. At some point, probably whilst crouching in the bottom of a foxhole, somebody hit upon the idea of speeding up a part of the internal working mechanism that had been frustrating everybody to date.

When they got home four of them pooled their savings – $50,000 in all – and set up a small company in what is now known as Silicone

Valley. Success was instant and phenomenal and several years later they were bought out for an unbelievable fortune. Alan and Lorraine now enjoy life to the full and we are delighted that they chose to spend a few days of it here with us.

Just occasionally we still find ourselves thrown by the unexpected. One evening we and our other guests were sitting having supper waiting for the new arrivals to put in an appearance. Eventually a matt black Mercedes with darkened windows crept up the drive and came to a halt. The driver, a youngish man with a foreign accent, came up the steps and introduced himself.

Behind him was a slim young girl who, through her bashful smiles, we could see was wearing a brace and who was dressed in something akin to a gym slip, white socks and sandals. She was introduced as the wife and, with childish giggles and a lisp, she announced that they were tired and would like to go straight up to bed. It was just eight-thirty.

The scene was digested in total silence by those around the table until eventually someone said slowly and in a measured tone that, with the best will in the world, the child could be no more than fourteen – at the very most! A brief moment of panic as we visualised the arrival of an outraged father with a van load of his biggest friends or, worse still, the gendarmes acting on information received. But what could we do? We sat and thought about it for a minute or two, had a large drink and decided to play dumb innocence to any drama that chose to unfold.

That, I have to say, was an exceptional situation and most of our guests are quite, quite normal. They come for a few days or a week, sometimes longer. All seem to have fallen for this corner of France and the longer we are here the more fascinated we too have become. We now regard this small part of the countryside as our home territory and take great pride in helping our visitors find their way around, their enjoyment giving us much pleasure.

It is steeped in history and, as the ancient landmarks suggest, was popular in Roman times. Narbonne, as I mentioned earlier, was a principal port of entry and the main route inland to the north and west was the line of the great valley past Carcassonne, Castelnaudary to Toulouse before running on to Montauban, Agen and finally Bordeaux.

Tolosa, as Toulouse was then known, lies astride the River Garonne and, even now, one can see that the city had been built originally astride a major crossing point which the Romans would have used had they decided to move further west into the Gers. Had they continued downstream to the north-west they would have come to the point where the River Tarn joins the Garonne from the north. Sooner or later they would have explored up the Tarn valley, many opting to settle on the land where Gaillac stands today, developing the area into an important commercial centre.

If it was the Romans who made the first great impression here it was the Cathar movement, more than a thousand years later, that left an even greater mark on the countryside and local history. During the latter half of the twelfth century the whole region of the Midi was infiltrated by those preaching Catharism. Slowly at first but in ever-increasing numbers and with their confidence becoming ever stronger, the Cathars spread their gospel. Such was their impact on the population that many were converted to this new order and turned away from the Catholic church.

Eventually the Cathars and those they converted found themselves in direct conflict with King Philip of France and Rome. After years of fruitless dialogue Pope Innocent III called for a crusade against the Cathars, actively supporting the extermination of the movement. Throughout the early part of the thirteenth century a bloody campaign was waged by a number of warlords called in for the task.

The best known and perhaps the most infamous, was Simon de Montfort, Earl of Leicester who, along with others, put down the movement with unbelievable cruelty, all carried out in the name of religion. Many thousands were tortured and slain, usually burned. Lands were confiscated and the population forced back to the teachings of Rome.

One of the most bloody massacres of all was here in Lavaur. Once the town's defences had been breached the attacking force rounded up the inhabitants. The Maire of Lavaur – a woman named Dame Guiraude – was first tortured and raped before being thrown into the town well which was then filled up with rocks. Eighty knights and male defenders were then tortured and slain after which no less than 400 inhabitants were burned alive in great pits. No Geneva Convention or Charter of Human Rights then.

Now, centuries later, life is somewhat more peaceful but we have been left with many reminders of those dark days, from the magnificent cathedral at Albi and the smaller but no less beautiful cathedral of our own here in Lavaur, to the ruins of the Cathar strongholds often built in remote high spots in the Pyrenees.

Within a short drive are a number of hilltop bastide towns such as Cordes, Puycelci and Castelnau de Montmiral, built originally by local people to protect themselves not only from those who persecuted the Cathars, but from bands of robbers and brigands that roamed the area in those far-off times. These small towns are a delight to visit. Many of the buildings and much of the fortifications remain more or less in their original state externally, having been modernised carefully and in keeping with the architecture of the period.

We have not yet explored the Pyrenees thoroughly but, a few years ago, we took a few days off and drove down to Cauterets, a small spa town high in the mountains behind Lourdes. Close to the town are some of the highest peaks in the whole Pyrenean range and the French, who lay out their national parks so well, have created numerous well-signed walks into the mountains.

A short drive from the little spa town takes the traveller into the magnificent natural amphitheatre – Le Cirque de Gavarnie. Here, glaciers have gouged a great bowl out of the north face of the mountains, the peaks of which rise up to well over 10,000', towering more than 6,000' above the little village of Gavarnie in the valley below.

We were there in May, a perfect time to go when the cascades and waterfalls were full of ice-cold water rushing down from the snow line, the early migrant birds had returned and the hillsides were carpeted with wild flowers. The weather was glorious and each day we walked far into the mountains with our picnic lunch. Alone, save for the occasional walker and the soaring buzzards and eagles, we were enthralled by the majesty of the place.

Even for May the sun was hot and high up on the snow line we sat and ate lunch in just shorts and T-shirts before coming back down into the valleys where we cooled ourselves in the cold, clear water of the streams. We came away knowing that we had just touched the surface of the mountains and that we would, for sure, be back again.

And so this is the way it is here at Bosc Lebat. We have done much to our home and have had a grand adventure these last few years but there is still so much for us to do and see in the Tarn and the neighbouring Departments. Tristan did himself proud and passed his exams well. After taking a year off after the *lycée* to work as a student teacher at my old private school in southern England, he went up to Sheffield University.

All four of our sons are now in England and we are here on our own when the seasons are behind us. Already we are beginning to look at what might lie ahead. Our beautiful home needs all our time, our care and attention, allowing us little scope to venture further afield. We love it here and plan to stay on in this area for some years yet, but perhaps the time has come for us to think of a move.

It will be a hard wrench but who knows what lies around the corner. As I pen these final words, the dogs lie at my feet unaware of the thoughts passing through my mind. Outside, across the courtyard, the leaves of the vines are blood red along the *gîte* wall. It is now late afternoon and they are highlighted by the October sun – the same dazzling array of colours as I first saw almost forty years ago when canoeing down the Saone. The air is still, not a breath of wind, and it is as peaceful and as quiet as only Bosc Lebat can be. Shall we move on or shall we stay yet awhile? It is at times like this that I realise our love for France remains as strong as ever. Behind me on the wall, the calender for next year is up and already the first bookings are marked, so perhaps, after all, we will be here for some time to come.